Guided With
a
Steady Hand

Guided With

a

Steady Hand

*The Cultural Landscape
of a Rural Texas Park*

Dan K. Utley and James W. Steely

Baylor University Press
Waco, Texas

Dedicated to
Clay J. Davis,
educator, advocate, preservationist, friend

Library of Congress Cataloging-in-Publication Data

Utley, Dan K.
    Guided with a steady hand : the cultural landscape of a rural
Texas park / Dan K. Utley and James W. Steely.
        p.   cm.
    Includes bibliographical references (p.   ) and index.
    ISBN 0-918954-68-1
    1. Mother Neff State Park (Tex.)--History. 2. Neff, Pat Morris,
1871-1952. 3. Civilian Conservation Corps (U.S.)-- Texas--
Coryell County. 4. Coryell County (Tex.)--History, Local.   I.
Steely, James Wright.
    F392.C8U75   1998
    976.4'515--dc21   98-26499
                                                            CIP

Cover drawing from The Master Plan, Mother Neff State Park, Pat
Neff Papers, Texas Collection, Baylor University.

Printed in the United States of America on acid-free paper.

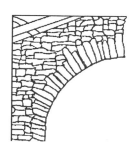

Contents

Foreword

The first time I visited the Mother Neff State Park was on the evening of 25 May 1984, when I camped beneath the boughs of some of the same trees nurtured there by Governor Pat Neff. I had been in the field all day, visiting abandoned towns and photographing them for a ghost town book I was writing, and I had just been taking photographs in the nearby community of The Grove. After a long day of picture making, interviewing, and note taking, I was ready for some rest. Having purchased some groceries earlier that afternoon, I followed the map and sign posts to Mother Neff State Park, which I had heard somewhere was the "first Texas state park."

After paying a nominal fee at the park entry, I found myself a grass-covered spot to camp beneath huge trees not far from a covered pavilion and there put my bright orange-colored pup tent. Having before been surprised while tenting by rain storms, I thought ahead that I might need to seek shelter beneath the nearby roof should I loose my lightweight tent that night in a thunderstorm. As events turned out, the evening was cloudless and calm, so I prepared my simple dinner using a close-by barbeque grill, and then I set out on foot in the dimming light to "see the park."

Walking up to and then into the open-sided concession building, I could see that it was by no means new. In fact, the old stonework in the twilight seemed even older than its 1930s construction. The style, however, reminded me of structures I had seen built by National Park Service personnel during the days of the New Deal. I could not get over the size and beauty of the big, open fireplace, and I wondered how many overnight groups over the decades had roasted wieners and toasted marshmallows there. Overhead were massive roof beams, which a bronze plaque on the wall recorded as having been hewn and placed there by members of the Civilian Conservation Corps. By this time, however, darkness had fallen, and bone-tired from a day in the field, I retired to my tent for a night of rest. The next morning I was up before dawn and in the car headed for the next ghost town site on my hit list. My first visit to Mother Neff State Park had come to its close, but I remembered it, and since then have returned time and again.

My most memorable subsequent revisits to Mother Neff State Park were with groups of Baylor University students who had signed up to take my historic preservation course at the school. Dan K. Utley generously agreed repeatedly to meet with the students in this class, and it became part of our expected routine to have one session take place with him at Mother Neff State Park. There Dan discussed with the students the theory and practice of cultural resource management, using the park as a teaching laboratory.

It was during these visits in the early 1990s that I learned I had not in 1984 indeed camped in the "first Texas state park," but rather a site that had masqueraded as such for half a century. More importantly, however, I learned of the significance of the Civilian Conservation Corps in the development of the core of Texas state parks during the days of the Great Depression. I began to look back on the many parks where I had camped before and started realizing that the CCC boys had built the shelters, entry station, and visitors' center I had enjoyed at the Palo Duro State Park near Canyon and Amarillo, had erected the concession building where since childhood I had bought pop at the Cleburne State Park near my hometown of Cleburne, and had constructed the wonderful pool where I had enjoyed swimming at the Abilene State Park outside Abilene. It all started coming together for me, and I began more fully to appreciate the contributions of the young men half a century before who had come from impoverished homes to undertake work for the public good in creating such places.

Dan also shared with my students an understanding of the sequence of human occupancy on the land. Walking over the lowland and upland areas of Mother Neff State Park, he showed them the actual physical evidence of prehistoric Texans, the early Euro-American settlers, late farmers, the CCC boys, and then of park administrators and visitors over the years. It was as if Dan were using Mother Neff Park as his textbook, while the students walking through the park "read" its evidence.

Sometime during this story I became acquainted with James W. Steely and his scholarly investigations into the role of the Civilian Conservation Corps in Texas state parks. Our first connections, however, were in a shared interest in the railway and engineering heritage of Texas. He subsequently collaborated with me in the preparation of several National Register of Historic Places nominations and worked with my Baylor University students in their semester projects in historic preservation. Several of the student-prepared NRPH nominations have been successful in reaching the state board of review. Jim had delved as deeply into the history of the CCC in Texas as Dan has into the specific past of Mother Neff State Park, and their shared collaboration has resulted in this fascinating study.

Most histories of communities and institutions examine them in isolation from the world around them, but not this one. The two authors have indeed looked in detail into the history of Mother Neff State Park. At the same time, however, they have explored the state and national context for their site-specific study, and in doing so have made Mother Neff State Park into a case study for Texas state parks in general. Only rarely do works such as this consider the highly important broader world in which events unfolded on the local level, but here the ideal may be found. I commend the efforts of the two authors.

As you read these pages, "breathe deep" the fresh air from its pages as you "listen" to the perching birds singing in the tree limbs above. Even better, take this little book along as you too enter the open-sided concession building at Mother Neff State Park and sit in front of the big, oversized fireplace. Savor the words in the place about which they are written. Even if you can't go to the park this weekend, still savor the words as you sit in your easy chair in front of your own fire . . . and plan your personal visit to Mother Neff State Park.

T. Lindsay Baker
Hillsboro, Texas

Preface

Roaming the Cultural Landscape

This is, at one level, simply the story of a park, one of the smallest in the Texas park system. It is the historical account of a "cultural landscape," a swatch of the earth that has hosted human cultures from prehistoric times to the present, and now portrays characteristics of both the natural and the refined. Thus, the story relates how people decided that a particular tract of rural farmland, the relatively unproductive, flood-prone river bottomland of a pioneer homestead near the center of the state, was worthy of preservation as a place of refuge and recreation for the public. It is also an account of related matters: planning issues, park operations, interpretation, viability of utility, and historic preservation.

Parks are not static features on the land. As cultural landscapes they are, in the best sense, dynamic, changing, and challenging. They reflect, in microcosm, certain guiding philosophies of society, from concepts of wilderness and nature to the demands of urban growth and environmental conservation. As society changes, so too does its institutions, including parks.

The lag in change may be slow—perhaps even at times barely discernible within a generation—but it is inevitable. Change over time is a broad and basic definition of history.

But, pull back from the fundamental history of a place, particularly one like Mother Neff State Park, and you soon find other dimensions to the story, as well as diverse contexts of understanding. There are the complexities of people, their decisions, their memories, their dreams, and their actions. There are the uncertainties of nature and the sometimes devastating examples of its ultimate power. There are also the significant elements of politics, architecture, and social change. And through it all, there are the perspectives, the individual frames of reference that drive decision making. Like a park itself, the perspectives are always dynamic, changing, and challenging.

Historians James West Davidson and Mark Hamilton Lytle ably addressed the significance of perspective in their book, *After the Fact: The Art of Historical Detection*. Writing specifically about the focused history of a place, or of local history, they noted:

> . . . a keen mind working on a small area will yield results whose implications go beyond the subject matter's original boundaries. . . . By understanding what has taken place on a small patch of ground, the historian can begin to see more clearly the forces shaping the larger historical landscape.[1]

This, then, is a local story told large. It is the history of one place as it was played out over time against a tableau of larger historical events. It is, in effect, history from the bottom up—part of the "new" social history that is now no longer so new. To paraphrase a speaker—whose name has long since been forgotten—at a local history symposium at the University of Texas over a decade ago: If a person studies nineteenth-century Texas, that's considered antiquarianism, but if a person studies eighteenth-century Paris, that's deemed scholarship. The difference, the speaker argued, could be found not in antiquity, but in perception and presentation.

The simple story of a little state park would not be without its merit on face value. After all, countless visitors to the park are unaware of even the major details of its development, and most have no idea of the significant role it played—and continues to play—in the history of the state park system. Some would even claim disinterest in the history of the place, yet their senses and their emotions cannot help but be heightened by the heritage, both natural and historical. On many planes, there are important personal associations with the park, whether perceived and analyzed or not.

Mother Neff State Park is everything a park should be. It is, by nature, an oasis, a place where geologic and environmental zones mingle without a clear sense of dominance. Prairie meadows of abundant wildflowers, grasses, prickly pear, and scattered shrubbery give way dramatically to steep and dark ravines, densely shaded by oak, pecan, willow, and junipers. Water forced from the uplands has carved the canyons, gouged out rockshelters, rearranged boulders, deposited rich alluviums in the crags, sculpted terraces, and then continued on its way to the Leon, the Brazos, and the Gulf of Mexico.

Culturally, Mother Neff State Park represents a continuum of civilization that reaches from prehistoric times to the present. For millennia, people have roamed its prairies, camped beneath its canopy, built fires to illumine its darkness, sought refuge in its natural shelters, fished its waters, and fled from its river torrents. And the people have also left evidence of their existence, from eons of burned rock and meandering trails to cattle fences and playground equipment.

Seeking rest, refuge, and perhaps rejuvenation, people have looked to the park as a source of inspiration, both spiritual and natural. For generations, people have gathered in the park to enjoy quality time with their friends and families, to celebrate history, to hear beautiful music and intriguing speakers, to talk about community building, to honor motherhood, to offer the occasional burnt sacrifices of hot dogs and marshmallows, and to sing the praises of God and baptize believers. They have also laughed and cried, whooped and hollered, and snored and sighed.

People have come alone to wander the trails, to photograph the wildflowers, to pray, and to revel in solitude. Some may have come seeking a renewal of spirit or a safe harbor in which to relieve the daily stress. People have also come in pairs and talked of love and beauty and nature and the future. Beneath the expansive park canopy, governors and senators have gathered. So have farmers, schoolchildren, civic groups, college societies, scout troops, pecan pickers, churches, laborers, park officials, industrial workers, soldiers, conservation corpsmen, and multiple generations of family.

But, throughout the ages the people have been primarily visitors. At best, they have been only temporary tenants on the land. They have always had to share the park with its native inhabitants. Buffalo once moved across its prairies in massive herds, virtually unchecked and uncaring. On the margins were the wolves and the wildcats, now, like the buffalo, also part of the past. Today, the park is largely the domain of smaller critters who leave their distinctive tracks nightly in the muds of the

Leon flats. Squirrels, deer, possums, raccoons, mice, and rabbits ably represent the furred set, but there are also the frogs, salamanders, turtles, and snakes, berattled and otherwise. Additionally, there are the fish, whose presence is often made known only with a ripple, a faded shadow, or a special appearance at the end of a line. There is also the ubiquitous armadillo, whose aborted dig sites can be found throughout the grounds, the birds that stretch the upward dimensions of the park, and an occasional coyote, spotted only in fleeting glimpses as it makes its way quickly across a road or open prairie.

And there is history. There are the memories of a young man roaming the hills in Victorian times, storing up the inspiration he later drew upon when, as governor, he spoke eloquently and almost incessantly about parks with the personal passion necessary to bring about change. There were the chautauquas that brought people together for entertainment and education. There was the Great Depression, when people were forced to reassess their traditional ties to the land. There were also the young men and the leaders of the Civilian Conservation Corps who made their presence known by a dramatically altered landscape, while also utilizing nature to soften the impact. There were rumors of war, followed by the actualities of war, that affected even a simple little park in Central Texas. There were the weekend dances, where strains of swing and rock and roll competed with the shrill notes of songbirds. There were the revivals, the Mother's Day celebrations, the camporees, and the community picnics. And there were the floods that moved the place to center stage in the continuing debate about the meaning and purpose of parks. Mother Neff State Park is everything a park should be.

Balancing the historical equation was a personality as strong and complex and contradictory as the land itself: Pat Morris Neff, farm boy, lawyer, Baptist, Texas governor, college president, state parks board founder, member, and chairman, park superintendent, activist, orator, overseer, and devoted son. Imbued with an unwavering sense of place that influenced his actions even as he walked the halls of power in Austin and Waco, Neff had an equally developed sense of his role in history. A handsome and impeccably tailored individual, with principles as precise and perhaps as starched as his collars, he reflected both the rigidity of Victorian times and the progressiveness of the future. He was obviously aware that he was a man for his time. With his noteworthy gift for oratory, he drew people to his philosophies from a common past and shared with them his own visions of promise and prosperity for the future.

Pat Neff drew great strength from his mother, and she was unquestionably at the core of his character throughout his life. Some considered him "mother-centric," but he never paled from his devotion to her. She was simply the most important figure in his life, and he honored her memory every chance he got. His words of dedication to her in a book of speeches showed, with remarkably florid prose, the depth of his devotion and his pride:

> To her who passed for me through the martyr-dom of motherhood; to her who during weary days and sleepless nights bent above my infant couch; to her who guided with a steady hand my erring feet from childhood to manhood; to her, first to see my virtues and last to see my faults; to her across whose brow the cutting cares of time have plowed deep furrows in which naught but beauty can be traced; to her on whose honored head the wintry winds of eighty-five years have flung the glittering snowflakes that never melt; to her from whose careworn hands

and around whose feeble feet the withered leaves of life's autumn are fast falling, but in whose heart still bloom the flowers of Spring; to her who during all these years has lived the simple faith of a simple life, far removed from the world's ignoble strife, the noblest and best woman in all the world because she is my mother, the thoughts contained within this book are hereby lovingly dedicated.[2]

So intense and pervasive was Neff's love for his mother that he often cloaked her obvious virtues with almost mythical reminiscences. Throughout his life, he was not one to let simple facts get in the way of a good story, and he knew a good story when he perceived one. Neff's penchant for hyperbole or myths most likely resulted more from dramatic emphasis or from convenience of memory than it did from deceit. Myth was to Neff as it was to Somerset Maugham, who described it as the "protest of romance against the commonplace of life."[3] The public memory of Isabella Shepherd Neff, the "mother" of Mother Neff State Park, is due largely to her son's craftsmanship as a wordsmith, image-spinner, and selective keeper of the family history. He genuinely loved his mother, and he protected her, even from the equality of her "simple life." Her simple gift of a few acres of land for a public gathering place—an honorable and meaningful gesture in its own right—thus became an inspiration for generations and a focal point of progressivism as a result of Neff's search for greater meaning. That does not diminish her actions; it only makes it more difficult to evaluate.

Students of Texas history will always remember Neff primarily for his two public lives—as politician and educator—and both are certainly worthy of further research and analysis. While this book will dwell to a limited extent on his accomplishments in both arenas, this is not intended as a political study or as a theological examination of a public man. The Pat Neff presented here is a man of focused purpose, with a park carved from his family farmstead serving as a lifelong point of action. The story of Neff and Mother Neff State Park cannot be told in a vacuum; it existed within various spheres of influence, from politics and power to myth and expediency. Throughout his life, Neff guided the park's development, significance, and history with a steady hand reminiscent of the one who had carefully led him "from childhood to manhood."

The genesis of this book was a casual conversation between the authors, longtime colleagues, about the lack of published material on the Civilian Conservation Corps in Texas. Both were aware of the role the organization played in the formation of Mother Neff State Park, and both, through their own independent research projects, knew of the impressive archival materials associated with the site. Perhaps no other state park in Texas has the depth and diversity of historical records, including CCC camp newspapers, oral histories, correspondence, newspaper clippings, historical photographs, vintage drawings, and archeological surveys. But the authors realized too that the abundance of documentation only served to enhance an otherwise unique story—the story of a New Deal-era park and the grand vision of a governor who was also the park's donor, benefactor, and promoter. In his mind, the park was either first or foremost, and the distinctions he made set the park's history for generations— even to the present day. Over the years, perceptions have often driven the story, but there have also been the realities with which to contend.

The authors came to this project with differing, yet complementary, perspectives. One, an architectural historian, had, through his office in the Texas Historical Commission, been instrumental in listing the park in the National Register of Historic Places. In his own research regarding park architecture and New Deal park policies, he had also come to appreciate the Mother Neff park for its significant role in the Texas story. The other author, a twentieth-century social historian, learned of the National Register nomination while serving on the board of review that approved the listing. But he became involved in the details of the park's history when he was commissioned to assist with a cultural resource management assessment for the Texas Parks and Wildlife Department. Both authors realized from the vantage of their different perspectives—from archaeology to architecture and from social change to recorded memories—that Mother Neff State Park was the ideal place to tell the microcosmic story of the CCC in Texas.

The authors are indebted to many people who helped them realize their objectives. First, there was the support of staff members at Baylor University, most notably Janet Burton, editor for Baylor University Press, and Ellen K. Brown, archivist for the Texas Collection. Both met with the authors early on and graciously listened to their ideas and encouraged their enthusiasm. Additionally, Mrs. Brown deserves special thanks for her capable assistance in research related to the papers of Governor Pat Morris Neff. Her skill and training as an archivist serve to complement her talents as an accomplished researcher, and the questions she asked of the authors helped direct this project in its initial stages. The entire staff of the Texas Collection, especially director Kent Keeth, provided invaluable assistance along the way.

Another very special person at Baylor has been Dr. Thomas L. Charlton, Vice Provost for Research for the university. Dr. Charlton is also the founder of the Institute for Oral History at Baylor, and it was through his office as director of that research center several years ago that he offered his assistance with the National Register nomination process and his support of a staffer's interviews with E. L. "Pete" Carpenter, longtime park superintendent. Dr. Charlton understands and appreciates the literature of memory, and this book hopefully is richer for that lesson learned in his employ.

Pete Carpenter was only one of many officials with the Texas Parks and Wildlife Department who assisted with this book. At the park, he was first interviewed in the superintendent's home not long after the devastating flood of 1992. Then only weeks away from his retirement, after many productive years as the park administrator, he began by lamenting its damaged condition. But, despite his disappointments at the time, he obviously realized the flood and his retirement were only part of the changes the park had experienced over the years. Its remarkable recovery in only a few short years is in many respects a tribute to both the healing hand of nature and the sincere efforts of people like Mr. Carpenter.

All of the park staff were helpful in providing research leads, park access, and encouragement. Without exception, they are some of the most dedicated people in public service for the state. Their friendliness and genuine enthusiasm are great tributes to the park system in general. Special recognition is due Superintendent John Roberts and his assistant, Charlotte Weiss. Mr. Roberts is a tireless worker and promoter, and his appreciation for the history of the park he serves is both compelling and infectious. Mrs. Weiss, who grew up in the area near the park, is no less enthusiastic about her work assignment. She has a special place in her heart for the men of Company 817 of the CCC, the septuagenarian and octogenarian "boys" who built the park. She has worked countless hours on her own time to gather stories, to preserve historical photographs, and to promote the annual CCC reunion each fall. Future generations will be forever in her debt for the work she has done to keep the history alive.

In Austin, there were several Parks and Wildlife personnel who helped with this project in special ways. Planner Bob Singleton provided information on recent plans for park development, and former planner John Williams made deed records available and provided important answers to tricky land ownership questions. A former historian with the department, Sue Winton Moss, years ago brought the agency's attention to the historical and architectural significance of the CCC parks, and her special inventory project assistant, Sarah Boykin, helped in myriad ways to document the parks and the various elements of their built environment.

Any acknowledgment of the Texas Parks and Wildlife Department in the preservation of Mother Neff would be incomplete without mentioning Dr. Cynthia Brandimarte, formerly with the Austin headquarters, who initiated the cultural resource management report that formed the nucleus of this work. It was her admonition early on that every effort should be made to tell the social side of the history that drove much of the initial research. Likewise, Ron Ralph, a recently retired archaeologist with the TPWD's regional office in Waco, provided important field assistance in matters related to both the cultural history and the archaeology of the park. While Dr. Brandimarte and Mr. Ralph are no longer in the employ of Texas Parks and Wildlife, their contributions to a better understanding of park history in the state remain a hallmark of their work with the agency.

With regard to the cultural resource survey of the park, special thanks are due Dr. Solveig Turpin, indefatigable director of the Borderlands Archeological Research Unit at the University of Texas at Austin. Under her direction, field researchers were given the necessary support to "get the story." Even when it outgrew project constraints and funding, she never let up. The result was a comprehensive report, *Mother Neff State Park: Prehistory, Parks, and Politics,* that covered the history, archaeology, and geology of the area's unique setting.

An equally important resource in the preparation of this book has been the Texas Historical Commission files related to the park's nomination to, and successful listing on, the National Register of Historic Places. Clay Davis, resident of the Old River Road area, provided the initial impetus, as well as much of the research and writing. Among those assisting him in achieving his objective were Tory Laughlin Taylor, Lisa Hart-Stross, and Charles Peveto of the THC, and employees of the Waco office of the Texas Department of Transportation.

A number of people unselfishly assisted with both the research and review of this manuscript. Special thanks are due Dorothy Blodgett of Austin and David Scott of Gatesville, who graciously provided access to their on-going and exhaustive research of Pat Neff. Their insights and perspectives reassured the authors of the significance of the Mother Neff story, while also influencing new angles on their research design. Dr. T. Lindsay Baker, an eminent historian who grew up near a CCC park at Cleburne and who deeply shares the authors' interests in the social, cultural, and architectural history of Texas, provided both encouragement and direction for this project. Because of the sincere respect both authors have for Dr. Baker as a friend, mentor, colleague, and counselor, it was fitting that he be asked to provide a foreword to the book, which he graciously agreed to provide. The authors are indebted to him for much more than his kind comments.

Research for this book took the authors to numerous collections, in addition to those already mentioned. Along the way, they were assisted by countless staff members who gave of their time and expertise, perhaps never realizing their efforts would someday result in a published history. Among those who have earned our gratitude in that regard are the employees of the county clerks' offices in Gatesville and Waco who provided answers and directions about important land title and probate research. Equally helpful were the staffs of the National Archives and Records Administration and the National Park Service, especially those in the office at Harper's Ferry, West Virginia.

And finally, there are two groups—both select and special— without whom this work would not have been possible. Their direction and inspiration far overshadow that of anyone else associated with the project. First, and perhaps foremost, are the "boys" of Company 817 of the Civilian Conservation Corps. This is essentially their story. Raw and untamed as the land they worked in the depths of the Great Depression, they rose to the occasion, and both benefitted from their efforts. Most of the CCC enrollees are gone now, and many of those that remain still gather in the park to reminisce about the "Happy Days." Hopefully, each has recognized at some point in his post-camp life that their existence made a difference. They suffered hardships, but they proved, like the unofficial motto of the CCC,

"We Can Take It." Generations of Texans are glad they did. Countless park visitors over many decades have rested in the shade of the trees the CCC planted. They have walked their trails, crossed their bridges, and marveled at the craftsmanship of their buildings. Once people have heard the CCC story, it is impossible to visit the parks—one of the most visible reminders of the organization's existence—without thinking about the boys. If this book in any way honors their sacrifices and accomplishments, and passes their stories along to new generations, it is only a minor memorial that pales in comparison to the legacies they have bequeathed to all of us—enduring reminders of the public good that often comes from providing others a helping hand in time of need.

And every son or daughter knows exactly what "guided with a steady hand" means in reference to his or her mother. So many things in our culture, just as in Pat Neff's era, allow us the privilege of exploring our personal limits, and to search freely for our adult place in life. Our mothers, more than any other factor, establish resonable bounds for that exploration and search. They keep us focused, and they convey the consequences of not observing the Golden Rule. Few of us achieve a governor's level of public forum to thank our parents, much less to name a state park for them, but we all feel the same. So, in the spirit of Pat Neff, we offer our abiding love and thanks to our mothers, Mabel Prater Utley and Jane Record Steely.

Dan K. Utley and James W. Steely
Austin, Texas
January 1998

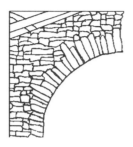

1

Embracing Change

Pat Morris Neff understood transition. It was part of his environment, his genealogy, his personal history, and his professional career. It influenced his understanding of Texas, it marked his greatest successes, and it defined the strongly held philosophies that were at the core of his existence. To Neff, transition was something to be embraced, not avoided or feared. It was not, however, something to be sought at any cost. He eschewed change for the sake of change. Neff's world of transition was gradual, deliberate, systematic, meaningful, and progressive.

The land into which Neff was born in 1871 was clearly one of change, historically as well as geologically. Coryell County, in Central Texas, is located near the 98th meridian, a global north-south line that Western historian Walter Prescott Webb referred to as an "institutional fault." To Webb, the meridian was a general demarcation that denoted significant change when overlaid on traditional historical patterns of westward migration and settlement. He viewed it as an imprecise, but cultur-

ally discernible, transitional zone between the dominant tim-
berland settlement of the eastern United States and the Great
Plains that characterized the dramatically different landforms
of the American West:

> At this fault the ways of life and of living changed.
> Practically every institution that was carried across
> it was either broken and remade or else greatly al-
> tered. The ways of travel, the weapons, the method
> of tilling the soil, the plows and other agricultural
> implements, and even the laws themselves were
> modified.[1]

Webb added that those who brought their "institutions" to the
area along and west of the 98th meridian "were thrown by
Mother Necessity into the clutch of new circumstances."[2]

Webb's frontier line was, in effect, a response to the question that has long puzzled U. S. historians: Where does the
American West begin? And perhaps the broader question had
always been: What is the American West? Historian Frederick
Jackson Turner stirred considerable debate, which continues to
enfold his work to this day, about the cultural and historical
role of the American frontier. Turner's monumental "frontier
thesis," which he delivered as an essay at the Columbian Expo-
sition in 1893, came at a time when government agencies, the
media, scholars, and interpreters of American culture generally
observed the end of the frontier and the closing of an important
chapter of U. S. history. His thesis was, essentially, that those
general elements that characterized American civilization—most
notably independence, democracy, and free enterprise—reached
their true defining moments as a part of the westward migration. As Americans moved farther from the European-influenced

eastern coast, Turner argued, the more American they became. As he noted, "The existence of free land, its continuous recession, and the advance of American settlement, explain the American development."[3]

Although Turner wrote in general terms of change over time and physical space, and although he wrote specifically about the first American frontiers—the places immediately west of the Appalachians—his theory also addressed successive frontiers, including the one that affected the prairies of Central Texas in the mid-nineteenth century. Turner did not offer a specific line of change, as Webb would decades later, but he did speculate, symbolically at least, about points from which the sweeping change might have been observed:

> Stand at Cumberland Gap and watch the procession of civilization, marching single file—the buffalo following the trail to the salt springs, the Indian, the fur-trader and hunter, the cattle-raiser, the pioneer farmer— and the frontier has passed by. Stand at South Pass in the Rockies a century later and see the same procession with wider intervals between.[4]

In that vast area between Cumberland Gap and South Pass in a century of history, dramatic change occurred. Few could argue that the pioneers who crossed the Appalachians were identical to those who would push American civilization through the Rockies to the Pacific Coast. There were similarities, to be sure, with regard to political and social makeup, but there were also vast differences brought about primarily by the environment and by separation.

So, within the context of westward migration, where did the South end and the West begin? Where did Southerners become Westerners? Perhaps, as Texas historian Frank Vandiver noted, the answer can be found in the people as well as on the land. In a 1974 essay, "The Southwest: South or West?," he spoke of the human side of the migrational transitions espoused by both Webb and Turner. To Vandiver, the new breed of Southwesterners was the key to understanding the change. They were, he said, primarily people who were Southern in tradition and Western in vision.[5]

Two important Southern qualities Vandiver ascribed to the Southwesterners were a respect for history and a strongly developed sense of place. He noted:

> . . . there is a feel for kin that runs through the Southern story, a response of blood that seems to suffuse parts of Southern life with a haunting feel of home, of place. Place is a vital touchstone to the understanding of Southerners.[6]

In contrast, the Western influence on the human equation came from independence. Historically, Westerners were, he observed, "clearly self-reliant folk by necessity. A man was accepted at his human value and a poignant comradeship of survival bonded the thin line of pioneers."[7]

Within this grand zone of transition where the South gave way to the West, and where nineteenth-century pioneers presaged evolving lifeways, significant elements of the American cultural continuum were played out. Coryell County and the surrounding area have yielded considerable evidence of prehistoric existence. Archeological surveys at such places as Mother Neff State Park and nearby Fort Hood have identified rock shelters, lithic procurement areas, and terrace middens of burned rock and mussel shells of great antiquity. Some of the concomitant artifacts date from the Archaic Period, or roughly several thousand years BC to around 800 AD. Many more, however, are representative of the Late Prehistoric Period that followed, through the mid-sixteenth century, when the first written accounts of Texas marked the beginning of the Historic Period in the state.[8]

Native Americans still populated the present Coryell County area when Anglo-American settlers began moving there in the years following the 1836 Texas Revolution. Pioneer accounts indicate they were primarily members of the Tonkawa confederacy, although there are also historical references to the Comanche, Caddo, and Kickapoo. The Tonkawa were probably displaced from their ancestral Oklahoma homeland by the Apache around the seventeenth century. Principally followers of the buffalo, they had settled in Central Texas by the eighteenth century and begun to localize their subsistence along such rivers as the Leon and the Brazos. They would later be displaced farther south by the Comanche and Wichita, settling between the San Antonio and Trinity rivers.[9]

With cultural contact came cultural conflict, and settlers moving into the prairie regions of Central Texas demanded military protection as they pressed the frontier line westward. In 1839, Captain John Bird and Captain George B. Erath led Republic of Texas ranger forces into the area in a punitive expedition against Indians suspected of Milam County raids. The two groups skirmished first in Bell County, near the town of Little River, where Bird was a casualty of the fighting. Erath assumed command of the pursuit and continued it into present Coryell and McLennan counties. To anchor the frontier line temporarily, the rangers established an outpost called Fort Station along a Leon River tributary later known as Station Creek.[10]

With the annexation of Texas in 1845, the government of the United States inherited the "frontier problem." The first solution offered was a line of frontier defenses stretching across the state—and Central Texas—from the Rio Grande to the upper Trinity River area. One of the fortifications along that line was Camp Gates (later Fort Gates), established in 1849 east of present Gatesville, the seat of government for Coryell County.

The military presence in the area eventually resulted in the intended effect. The Indians and the settlers both moved farther west, while maintaining the invisible and shifting line of separation that marked the ever-changing frontier. Among those settlers who migrated to the area during this period of great transition were a newly-wed couple from Virginia, Noah and Isabella Shepherd Neff. Only a few days after their 1854 marriage in Roanoke, they began their westward trek to Texas, taking fifty-two days to reach Bell County. They resided there only three months before moving to land they purchased in Coryell County. They made their new home along the headwaters of Horse Creek on property originally patented to the heirs of Charles LaJoice in 1853.[11] The Neffs were apparently the first settlers to live on the land, a fact that perhaps later contributed to the family story surrounding Isabella Neff's gift of park land. "We got the title to that place from the Governor of Texas," she supposedly said, "and I don't see why I shouldn't just deed it back."[12]

Noah and Isabella Neff raised nine children on their Coryell County property near the rural community of Eagle Springs. Like their neighbors, they were subsistence farmers. Cotton was the principal, if not the only, regional cash crop. Despite growing conditions that were relatively less than ideal, given especially the state of agricultural technology at the time and the lack of adequate rainfall, cotton persisted. Against the odds, it was both a way of life and an economic necessity for those settlers from the Old South who migrated west to Central Texas in the antebellum period.

Historian Charles Ramsdell, in his seminal study of the natural limitations to slavery, noted that the western edges of Central Texas marked a significant barrier to viable cotton production in the years before the Civil War. Central Texas was then not only a social and cultural frontier, it was the frontier for the Southern cotton belt as well. Although there were limited exceptions, Ramsdell believed the dry climate, insect infestations, and stony soils that marked the transitional lands of the area also marked a barrier beyond which cotton—and thus slavery—would not have spread very far, even if the Civil War had not been fought.[13]

King Cotton was enough of a presence on the nearby prairies, especially in McLennan and Bell counties, and in the cultural history of the settlers, to secure its place in the lives of those who made their home the western edges of the transitional lands. It persisted well into the twentieth century, when it eventually gave way to the inevitable, and farmers began converting cotton fields to pasturage. During its reign, however, it was a determinant of settlement and culture in rural Texas.

Pat Neff was born into the dominant cotton culture transported from the Old South, and its presence had a lasting effect on his life. His words from an early speech delivered at the Texas Cotton Palace at Waco show his appreciation for the role the crop played in Texas. They also reveal his penchant for florid language, strong in regional imagery and evocative of universal human emotions:

When King Cotton tickles his Texas plantations
with its hoe, the world laughs, and when he has the
blues because it is too dry to plow, tears fall upon
the wrinkled shirt bosom of the human race. When
his tiny sprouts break the sod of early spring, with
the glory of the flowers of Ceylon, the current of
commerce courses the channels of trade with the
buoyant throb of a Hercules. As the stately stalk fruits
and flowers, the frenzied financiers of the world stand
on the tiptoe of speculative expectancy, and watch
the mercury of values rise and fall in the thermom-
eter of the world's wealth.[14]

Just as Neff knew the King Cotton of the South, he also
understood the Western Cattle Kingdom that followed it and
competed with farming for commercial attention. Although he
was born in 1871, at a time when cattle drives along the Texas
extension of the celebrated Chisholm Trail, east of Coryell
County, were on the wane, he frequently told stories about his
experiences with the droving cowboys. According to Emma
Morrill Shirley, his secretary who wrote a history of Mother
Neff State Park obviously drawing on her association with Pat
Neff for background, the family homestead was in the center of
the action:

Thousands upon thousands of cattle were driven by
the Neff homestead in the old days on their way to
the Kansas markets, and the dusty thirsty cowboys
always stopped for a drink from the spring and often for a piece of pie and a cup of coffee, brewed on
the back of Mother Neff's stove, where it is said a
pot of coffee simmered for more than forty years.

This stopping of the cowboys at his boyhood home gave rise to the favorite joke of Governor Pat M. Neff, that he learned the alphabet and how to read from the cattle brands on the herds that thundered by his very door.[15]

Neff himself noted in a speech dedicating a cowboy monument on the Capitol grounds in Austin:

> As a youth I lived on this trail [Chisholm], a hundred miles north of here, and many a day I watched the slow-moving, lowing herd, miles in length, pass by on its way from South Texas ranches to the markets and the ranges of the North.[16]

Given the years of his childhood and the imagery he used, especially the references to branded cattle, ranches, Northern ranges, and visiting cowboys, considerably west of the main Chisholm extension through Texas, Neff's memories were more likely reflective of early ranching than of cattle drives. Cattle were driven, no doubt, through the area to local markets, or even to railheads for shipment north. By the mid-1870s, however, free range in Central Texas was quickly giving way to fenced pastures and farms. Despite the inconsistencies, however, the imagery and myth of the American West clearly influenced Neff, as evidenced later in his dedicatory speech for the cowboy statue:

> The cowboy was brave. He had no sense of fear. He never forsook a friend in danger. He could draw quickly and shoot straight. He never hit in the dark. He never started east when he intended to travel west. He never failed to give instant battle

to an enemy. If vanquished, he always fell with
his back to the ground and his feet to the foe.[17]

Clearly, Neff reveled in the associational power of prose, and
the fact that his words might represent a transference of imagery to his own political character was not lost on him.

Pat Morris Neff not only understood transitions, he lived
them. Because of his sense of place and his own personal history, he could, therefore, be both Southern and Western. He
could be a country boy, but also travel the state in the newfangled automobile campaigning for office. He could be both
urban and rural, progressive and conservative, and stern and
gentle—all with equal effectiveness.

Like Vandiver's Southwesterner, Neff was influenced by both
the traditions of the past and the vision of the future. As a result, his campaign on behalf of such Progressive programs as
state parks was perhaps more effective. In his advocacy of a state
system of parks, he drew upon the impending transition most
people recognized, but which few were willing to accept. His
words were chosen not to exploit uncertainty, but to deal constructively with reality. And he called upon the public to embrace change, just as he had throughout his life:

> The call of the open country is ever a natural one of
> the human heart, and the massed life in the cities
> should never cause it to be crucified or to become
> dormant. . . . Camping and outing places, breathing
> spots for humanity, should be established along our
> highways throughout the State, at distances not
> greater than 100 miles apart.[18]

And Neff's goals were as personal as they were private, as evidenced in his long and tireless campaign to ensure that a small park carved from the family farm would be a worthy memorial to his mother, as well as a legacy for the people of Texas.

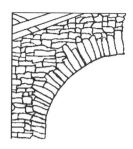

2

A Mother's Will and a Son's Way

Young Pat Neff's analytical mind and reverberating voice embellished a brief teaching career after 1894 upon receipt of his bachelor's degree from Baylor. But these qualities apparently energized greater ambitions, so he obtained in 1897 a law diploma from the University of Texas, then a master's degree from Baylor. With these newly combined personal and academic credentials, Neff won in 1898 a seat at the state legislature representing his broad Central Texas stomping ground.

The next year Neff married Baylor classmate Myrtle Mainer, and the 27-year-old lawmaker optimistically established his full-time legal practice, and family, with headquarters in Waco. Increasingly influenced through his third election by reform-minded legislators—and avowed Progressive governors Charles Allen Culberson and Joseph Draper Sayers—in January 1903 Neff parlayed the respect and support of his fellow representatives into selection as their Speaker of the House.

Though the youngest House leader on record, Neff retired after the session—common tradition in an era of single-term Speakers—and pursued law practice and family matters closer to home. The call to public service, however, once again moved Neff to the Democratic ballot, and from 1906 through 1912 he effectually served as McLennan County attorney. During those years, he claimed, friends in Austin repeatedly offered him a desk with the attorney general, but he declined in favor of politics woven within the booming cotton economy of Waco.[1]

Neff's early admittance to the Texas Capitol immediately followed a session highlighted by landmark legislation for historic San Jacinto battleground. After lengthy debate and intense lobbying in 1897 by the Daughters of the Republic of Texas, Neff's predecessors and Governor Culberson directed a $10,000 appropriation to preserve the site near Houston where Texans won their independence from Mexico in 1836. These funds helped create a sizable state preserve, adjacent to a ten-acre cemetery purchased fourteen years earlier as one of the state's first reservations for public recreation.

Unfortunately in the next three sessions—as Neff served in the House and as Speaker—aspiring Daughters could not obtain additional funds for roads and interpretive monuments at San Jacinto. Then in 1905—right after his retirement from the legislature—these women won a major victory by convincing Neff's successors to buy additional property at the Alamo in downtown San Antonio, and to acquire the historic Monument Hill cemetery near La Grange, holding casualties from the Dawson Massacre and the Mier Expedition. Finally, in 1907, Governor Thomas Mitchell Campbell signed a whopping $25,000 appropriation for major improvements at the Harris County battleground and naming this site "The San Jacinto State Park," the first property in Texas so-designated.

Interest in the state's legendary heritage only increased through 1911, the 75th anniversary of San Jacinto and Texas independence. That year lawmakers authorized appropriate observances and paid for the transfer of Stephen F. Austin's remains from Brazoria County to the State Cemetery in Austin. They also funded a sizable monument over the grave of Elizabeth Patton Crockett, widow of revolution-hero Davy Crockett, in Hood County. Somewhat tardy for the anniversary but animated by the commemorations, in 1913 citizens in Goliad County donated to the state a part of Fannin battleground, and the city of Gonzales transferred 150 acres of its municipal parkland to the state. These reservations, like San Jacinto and other state-owned historic sites became the responsibility of local committees designated by the governor.[2]

Meanwhile, Texas politicians trotted into the national spotlight with timely and crucial support of Woodrow Wilson for president. Through the maneuvering of Colonel Edward Mandell House—behind-the-scenes sponsor of governors Culberson, Sayers, Campbell, and others—forty Texans at the summer's national Democratic convention secured their party's nomination of candidate Wilson. As head of Princeton University, Wilson had developed his own mind and voice to become the foremost spokesman for the progressive movement, a coalition crossing party lines in support of social "reform" through strong and efficient government. Progressives—including Wilson's opponent Theodore Roosevelt leading a new Progressive Party—sought to direct the nation's prosperity and industrial might toward better living conditions for all Americans, including improved educational and recreational opportunities.

In the South and for Texas, Progressives particularly stood for limitations on big business and prohibition of alcoholic beverages. While the movement brought child-labor laws as well as state hospitals for the infirm, railroads and oil giants found their empires strictly regulated, and the liquor industry battled increasing attacks on its products. With Wilson's election that fall, he rewarded many of those "Immortal Forty" Texans from the Democratic convention with cabinet posts and other influential positions within the federal government. Progressive Texans in Washington, D.C., thus moved into the forefront of shaping America's political fortune.[3]

Ironically, as the liberal vision of Col. House moved from Austin to Washington, Texas state government sidestepped into an episode of Populism led in 1914 by newly elected Governor James Edward Ferguson. This ardent supporter of "plainfolk" admittedly extended some reformative hopes to tenant farmers and other poor Texans. But Ferguson stopped far short of supporting prohibition or women's voting rights, and he hesitated to offend big business or its lobbyists, including liquor agents. Luckily, in his first term Ferguson committed the progressive but politically benign act of supporting the addition of two more historical parks to the state's inventory. With a prolonged spirit of 1836, the city of Refugio donated its central plaza as King's State Park, named for Texas Revolution martyr Amon Butler King. The legislature and Ferguson also appropriated $10,000 to purchase fifty acres where the Texas Declaration of Independence had been signed, at Washington-on-the-Brazos in Washington County.

Again, local park commissions assumed responsibility for these sites presented as "state parks" in name only.

In 1916 Governor Ferguson headed the committee that visited Washington-on-the-Brazos and closed on new state parkland there. Favorable publicity for such gestures helped him win a traditional second term (every Texas chief executive since Reconstruction had served two bienniums) and during the 1917 session he signed a momentous bill creating the Texas Highway Department. But that summer Ferguson angered a growing political assembly of prohibitionists, then recklessly insisted on his personal reorganization of the University of Texas. Amid corruption charges and revelations of large contributions from the liquor lobby, Ferguson resigned just as the legislature impeached him and declared the ousted populist ineligible for public office.[4]

At this time, America's deepening commitment to the World War caused Texas state government, and replacement-Governor William Pettus Hobby, to maintain relatively low profiles for the duration. However, Hobby's unexpected elevation from lieutenant governor came with fortunate timing for Progressives, as he called a special session in spring 1918 to ratify the nation's alcohol-prohibition amendment, and to grant Texas women voting rights in state primaries. The next year, during regular session, lawmakers responded to war's end through ratification of the national woman-suffrage amendment. And recently re-elected Governor Hobby championed government efficiency through creation of the State Board of Control. This new agency assumed administration of all state purchasing, printing, building design, and eleemosynary hospitals and institutions. The Board of Control also took central responsibility for state historical grounds, including the five existing "state parks" at Fannin battleground, Gonzales, Refugio, San Jacinto, and Washington-on-the-Brazos.

Although Hobby ran only once for election as governor, his service through most of two bienniums fulfilled the two-term tradition and in 1920 he signaled a return to private newspaper management. By then the dismissal of Col. House from Wilson's Progressive circles, the lingering aftermath of Ferguson's removal, and Hobby's abrupt departure caught Texas Democratic leaders without a favorite son to place in the Governor's Mansion. Further, while alcoholic beverages now disappeared from American store counters and women celebrated their hard-earned right to vote, the nation also suffered a widening crime wave, severe racial discord, and plummeting prices for farm goods, especially cotton. The resulting political atmosphere called for a law-and-order candidate who also could cajole the Texas culture and economy into a renewed spirit of optimism and accomplishment.

Thus Pat Morris Neff decided his time had come to enter the race for governor. The Waco attorney with strong leadership credentials and knowledge of local and state governments donned his winged collar, string tie, and frock coat, fired up his aging Model T, and crisscrossed the state in a dusty one-vehicle campaign. Neff now perfected his rock-ribbed image of a nineteenth-century country statesman, while clearly embracing industrial populism as the first candidate to campaign over the state's patchwork highways via automobile. By the June primary he had driven 1,700 miles and earned a runoff with conservative ex-U.S. Senator Joseph Weldon Bailey. That summer, when his campaign rolled through the last county—one of thirty-seven in Texas never before visited by an aspiring or seated governor—Neff claimed to have driven more than 6,000 miles on his crusade.[5]

Neff defeated Bailey in the August runoff, carrying a healthy mandate for his platform of education, highways, and soil and water conservation. He pledged a drastic reduction in convict pardons, plus firm enforcement of prohibition and women's voting rights. Further, the candidate's use of an automobile bellowed much louder than words as he demonstrated independent movement from the state's heretofore monopoly rail network. Neff's politics and energy inspired Texans to vote strongly for a Progressive ticket that November, sweeping him into office and endorsing national Democratic candidates James Middleton Cox for president and his running mate Franklin Delano Roosevelt. However, Texas once again found itself out of step with the nation, as Republican candidates Warren G. Harding and Calvin Coolidge beat Cox and young Roosevelt.

Shortly after the victory, governor-elect Neff received an invitation to attend a National Conference on Parks in January 1921 in Des Moines, Iowa. His own inauguration would conflict with the park meeting dates, but more important, Neff apparently knew nothing of this national movement to encourage state park systems, and he sent no one to represent Texas per its hosts' suggestion. On January 18, 1921, as hundreds of enthusiastic park delegates returned from Des Moines to their twenty-five home states and eighty-four cities, Governor Neff rose once again in the Texas House of Representatives. From the Speaker's podium he outlined his vision for the session and for the coming decade.

> Texas furnishes an inviting field for constructive legislation. Nowhere could you find a land more conducive to the building of a high and enduring civilization than here where falls the light of the Lone Star. Not only is Texas a land of opportunity, but

ours is a day of opportunity. Let no one throw himself across the track to block the train of progress.
Obstructionists never win battles. It is the progressive, dynamic leader that counts. You, gentlemen of
the Legislature, are privileged to be the spokesmen
of a progressive and forward-looking people.[6]

Regretfully Neff's lofty rhetoric quickly stalled in a legislature full of divisive camps and disgruntled members disappointed
not to find Joe Bailey in the governor's office. When the regular
session ended in March, Neff found his Progressive platform all
but toppled, and a new budget as-yet undetermined. He sent
lawmakers home to cool off for a few months.

Then, on May 18, 1921, the governor's mother passed away
shortly after her 91st birthday. The family matriarch—a widow
since 1882—had moved to Austin with son Pat, where she ap-
plauded his inaugural speech from a wheelchair in the House of
Representatives, and lived briefly in the Governor's Mansion
with the first family.

With both his fervent progressivism and intense maternal-
ism badly shaken that spring, the governor suffered a level of
devastation only a politician could know: public indignity com-
pounded by private sorrow. "[T]o her who, during all these
years," Neff wrote of his pioneer mother six years earlier, reprinted on her death by the *San Antonio Express*, " has lived the
simple faith of a simple life, far removed from the world's ignoble strife, the noblest and best woman in all the world. . . ."
The generous obituary also pointed out that Mother Neff raised
her family, including youngest son Pat, in a "small log house on
premises still owned by Mrs. Neff at her death. . . ."[7]

Indeed, Mother Neff's will, written in 1916 with Pat Neff's
assistance, bequeathed a small part of the homestead as a "park

to the public, for religious, educational, fraternal and political purposes." The shaded clearing on the Leon River to which she referred had long served as a public gathering place, particularly for summertime camp meetings and community reunions. Her will further instructed son Pat as executor to erect a fence around the small unsurveyed plot, and to construct a "substantial Building in the nature of a Pavilion," along with "an archway [with] the name of the park, some what as follows: 'The Neff Park.'" [8]

Governor Neff left no confirmation of immediate political epiphany after his mother's death and reading of her will, though he later claimed this "Neff Park" donation first shaped his idea for state parks. In this light the bequest clearly offered a major plank for rebuilding his damaged gubernatorial platform in 1921, yet other events and initiatives that spring and summer likely adjusted Neff's political agenda as well. The first National Conference on Parks signaled a formal effort by the National Park Service and supporters specifically to help state governments start or improve their park systems, and Neff's office received summaries of the January meeting. Closer to home, a month before Isabella Neff's death, the "Davis Mountain State Park Committee"—including the region's state representative— had met to launch a campaign for creating a state or national park in these magnificent West Texas peaks and valleys.

As Neff called legislators back into session in July to complete appropriations and other unfinished business, an internal resolution called for lawmakers to investigate the Davis Mountains for park potential. Representative W. W. Stewart of Balmorhea and Senator Richard M. Dudley of El Paso pushed the measure to passage in August, with Neff's only recorded participation an expressed dissatisfaction over makeup of the investigating committee. In September some twenty of the legislature's most influential members set out on a train and auto trip that greatly expanded the Davis Mountains itinerary to include Palo Duro Canyon in the Panhandle, plus sites along the Frio River west of San Antonio. While this week-long excursion proceeded as planned and excited many West Texans along the way, its elected participants and their governor quietly entered the coming winter with no new public initiatives.[9]

In April 1922, Neff assisted the powerful good-roads lobby through an organizational meeting in Austin, and agreed to support a more effective Texas Highway Department during his coming second campaign. In May, Neff dispatched Mrs. James (Katie) Welder of Victoria—an officer in the Texas Federation of Women's Clubs for its statewide efforts in conservation—to attend the second National Conference on Parks in New York. Finally, in June, the governor traveled to Plainview for his first reelection speech, whereupon he suddenly and brilliantly connected the issues of automobiles and public recreation.

> [T]he state should establish parks, both large and small, throughout her borders. The people should have the breathing spots where they can enjoy nature in stream and tree, in rock and rill. We should have way-side parks and stopping places along our highways.[10]

Neff's second-term election strategy prevailed in the July primary, following tradition, and he spent the summer hammering a tight-fitting new platform. Upon the momentum of his now successful good-roads and way-side parks angle, he fueled throughout the summer ambitious land-reclamation proposals at large conventions of engineers and conservationists. Shortly after he captured the November election by wide margin, a much wiser Governor Neff assembled various supporters for his upcoming legislative program.

To lobby for a specific state parks bill, Neff identified David Edward Colp of San Antonio, a promoter of the good-roads movement, auto and road-bonds salesman, and one-time license director at the Texas Highway Department. Colp established an unofficial Texas Parks Association and upon its letterhead launched a broad mail solicitation asking cities along highway routes to donate roadside fishing and camping grounds as "state parks." While casting a huge net for small-park donations, Colp's campaign unfortunately did not coordinate with the Davis Mountains proponents, and, most importantly, it failed to secure public assistance from members of the legislature.

In the 1923 regular session, Neff faced even more divided and resistant legislators than those of his first-term experience. Yet he managed to capture a one-cent-per-gallon gasoline tax to fund the highway department, and to sell his conservation idea of a statewide engineering survey that would cost a staggering $600,000 (to be matched with federal funds). Holding the legislature into May through two called sessions, Neff scheduled a "special message" to lawmakers in preparation for his new parks bill. With practically no fanfare the 1921 park-investigation committee also submitted its report, but this stage was reserved only for the governor. "Nothing is more conducive to the happiness and contentment of a people," the governor broadcast on May Day in the House chamber, "than for them to go 'back to nature,' where the bees hum, the birds sing, the brooks ripple, the breezes blow, the flowers bloom and the bass bite."

> The health, welfare and happiness of the people
> of Texas is largely enhanced by the number of places
> within her borders where the people in vacation and

leisure periods can go for rest, recreation and relax-
ation. . . .

These primeval and picturesque places of native
charm and characteristic beauty are rapidly disap-
pearing before the onward march of cold, consum-
ing commercialism. . . .

By establishment of a system of parks and camping places throughout the State, we will make of Texas
the Mecca of auto tourists and bequeath to poster-
ity a most valuable legacy. . . .[11]

Neff's words formed the basis of a draft bill introduced
the next day, at last forging a link between Colp's heavily
promoted way-side parks and the Davis Mountains lobby
for a potential half-million-acre park. Still missing, curiously,
was a logical connection to the existing five "historical parks"
managed by the Board of Control. Exhausted legislators on
May 15 passed a somewhat diluted bill, and the exhausted
governor accepted their modifications, creating a new parks
board but calling only for inspections and donations, with
$1,500 (to be administered by the Board of Control) for travel
during the coming biennium.

There is hereby created a State Parks Board of
five members to be appointed by the Governor. . . .

Said board shall solicit donations to the State of
tracts of land, large or small, to be used by the State
for the purpose of public parks. . . .

The said parks board is especially directed to
inspect the Davis Mountains in Jeff Davis County,
to determine its feasibility as a park that might be
made a National Park. . . .[12]

With his new State Parks Board effective in September, Neff
that fall named its five members, beginning with Colp and adding further regional and organizational representations for the
balance. He recruited Hobart Key of Marshall to push for a
park at Caddo Lake; Mrs. W. C. Martin of Dallas to tap her
writing connections with the powerful *Dallas News*; Phebe K.
Warner of Claude for her established network of newspaper
columns and support of Palo Duro Canyon; and Katie Welder
of Victoria for her South Texas influences and recent attendance
of the national forum on state parks. Proving his interest in and
solicitation for the influence of newly enfranchised women vot-
ers, Neff deliberately chose the three females—a majority of the
board—from the ranks of powerful regional and state women's
organizations.

An intense winter publicity effort followed, during which
the board defined ideal donations for state parks as "beauty spots"
beside major highways, with fishing and camping opportunities for overnight motorists. In March 1924 Neff named Colp
chairman, and as the salesman's expertise in organizing barn-
storming auto caravans came to play, Neff set off with the board
from San Antonio on their initial "inspection trip." The governor made a bumper speech in Beeville, recording the "first"
donation of a 128-acre wooded municipal campground on the
highway. Following a few more speeches that week through eighteen counties along 1,500 miles, Neff and the board received a
dozen more donations and pledges.

During a subsequent caravan, the community of Boerne
northwest of San Antonio, promptly named its donation "Hallie
Maude Neff State Park" in honor of the governor's daughter,
who was driving his car that day in the caravan. At Van Horn
one Sunday, inside a packed hall of park supporters, Neff gave

his usual humming bees and singing birds sermon, adding, "When we serve humanity we serve God. We have no scruples about talking parks on the Lord's Day."[13]

In October, acting in his last few months as governor to ensure improvements at some of his new "state parks," Neff orchestrated a strange performance between the highway department and the prison system. The former supplied a World War-surplus truck plus tents and camping gear, and the latter assembled a group of convict "trusties" as labor for park work. To the great frustration of board chairman Colp, who hoped to assign this unusual park maintenance crew to sites along his favored highway routes, Neff's fleeting timetable allowed the trusties to improve only two parks that fall. Boerne's Hallie Maude Neff State Park supposedly became a priority when local citizens provided cash for cement and other building materials. And at "the Neff Park in Coryell County," Colp reported reluctantly, "[t]he citizens of that Community made up quite a bit of money and they are having an auditorium built. . . ."[14]

On the State Parks Board's final trip, in December, from Caddo Lake through North Texas, Neff's absence caused a dramatic reduction in local reception crowds and site donations. Still, by year's end the governor claimed more than fifty offers from Canadian to Brownsville, and from Big Spring to Palestine. Neff joined board members in Fort Worth, and accompanied their return trip south with a brief stop in Belton. There, his newly elected successor, Miriam Amanda Wallace Ferguson, along with her husband, ex-Governor Jim, hosted a reception for the outgoing executive and his parks board. The "Governors Ferguson," as some called this odd couple of Texas politics, made no promises that night, but Neff and Colp left with an impression that the new regime would support their next step: a bill in the legislature to accept a year's worth of parkland donations.[15]

In January 1925 Pat Morris Neff prepared to leave the Governor's Mansion just as the new legislative session began and just before Miriam and Jim Ferguson would move back after a seven-year absence. Miriam had surprised most Texans first with her unorthodox candidacy—since Jim was barred from holding public office she offered "two governors for the price of one" in her speeches—and by her victory, partly a result of Neff's failure to identify his own successor. Now, with a sweeping turnover in the legislature and an even stronger conservative shift in its membership, Neff drafted a farewell address that desperately appealed for continuation of his Progressive initiatives.

The twin subjects of state parks and highways consumed much of his speech, regrettably presented by proxies in the House and Senate chambers, but reprinted in the *Dallas News* and other newspapers the next day. Neff opened his park section with the usual staggering personal statistics: in the previous year he had traveled with the parks board "8,150 miles, visited eighty-two counties and spoke in behalf of the undertaking 110 times."

> What we want in Texas is a great system of State-owned parks, adjacent to our principal highways, at least one such park for every 100 miles of journey. This would encourage Texans to see Texas first and would be a great inducement and forceful invitation to tourists from other States to see our State.

In virtually his last gesture as governor, Neff recommended that the long list of site donations be accepted, then improved with a $50,000 appropriation, and designated "a part of the highway system" for management. Of the sixty-two parks on his list, Mother Neff Park, at ten acres, appeared among the smallest; most were in the 50- to 100-acre range, but soaring to a potential 7,000 acres in the Guadalupe Mountains. Neff further identified possible parks on state prison and school lands, and finally acknowledged the existing state historical parks, asking that "small portions of San Jacinto Battlefield Park, Goliad [meaning Fannin] Historical Park and Washington-on-the-Brazos park be set aside as camping grounds."[16]

The legislature would have none of it, and no sponsor could be found for the draft bill that presented Neff's recommendations. Worse, the *Dallas News* followed its report of the outgoing governor's speech with scathing criticism of the whole proposal. "It appears, from Governor Neff's message," the newspaper charged, that critical parts of the 1923 parks law "were ignored. No report was made on the Davis Mountains, except that Governor Neff described them as beautiful. The board seems to have devoted itself exclusively to the purpose of initiating a string of tourist camps, for commercial purposes." Adding insult to injury, the Senate Finance Committee chairman, Neff's fellow Waco resident Edgar E. Witt, introduced a resolution to return all the park donations, in effect killing the State Parks Board and Neff's movement.[17]

When the legislature went home in March, citizen Neff seemingly departed the battlefield for good; he resumed his law practice and accepted a commission from the new governor as head of an education survey. Over the next few weeks a dazed D. E. Colp stumbled in and out of government offices trying to piece together the recent quick and cruel series of events. He found some good news and more bad news: Witt's resolution had never been signed, so the parks board still lived, albeit in a state of suspension; but Governor Ferguson during this period had pardoned the convict park crew, and her new appointments to the state prison board refused to continue the arrangement. Colp now left the scene, as well, for more than a year, to recuperate and earn a living.

As the next legislative session of 1927 approached, Miriam Ferguson lost her bid for reelection (and broke the two-term tradition) to Daniel James Moody, Jr., the attorney general and symbol of newfound Democratic party unity. Neff and Colp resumed correspondence and shared optimism for support from Moody, but Neff insisted on a careful strategy for acceptance of the pending park donations only, not coupled with a request for funds. "I think we have had sufficient jolts along this line," he warned Colp. Then, just as the session began, Neff received an appointment from President Coolidge to the U.S. Board of Mediation that required a move to Washington, D.C. Colp found himself alone again on the battlefield.[18]

After an exhaustive winter of letter writing, Neff's surrogate at last secured assistance from women's groups and local park enthusiasts. Armed with a bona fide piece of legislation—a resolution introduced by Senator Margie Elizabeth Neal of Carthage, first woman to serve in the upper house—Colp one night found himself grilled before a Senate Finance Committee meeting headed by Edgar Witt. From some thirty communities still interested in hosting a state park, Colp held twenty-three detailed portfolios with photographs, plans, and improvement estimates on their tracts. Witt and his colleagues ultimately agreed to accept these twenty-three sites, on condition that no state funds be expended thereon, and their successful resolution declared that all "shall hereafter be known as state parks."[19]

In Colp's excitement throughout this hearing and in his immediate relay of events to Neff, the parks board chairman failed to realize that ten-acre Mother Neff Park in Coryell County did not make Witt's golden list. Perhaps Neff comprehended that in his own presumptive strategy he had never supplied a requisite portfolio on Mother Neff Park. Perhaps Neff understood that still more patience would be required before his mother's bequest could fulfill her son's dream of founding a "great system of State-owned parks."

Whatever Neff's thoughts or regrets in the spring of 1927, he continued to plan his own summer programs of speeches and reunions at the family's Leon River campground. Following the lead of several successful national outdoor forums, he personally established an annual series of "chautauquas" in the park. These special protracted events—named for the camp meeting grounds at Chautauqua, New York, where the most popular series originated in the 1870s—included speeches, plays, music, sermons, plus other diversions and entertainment. A program for his 1928 summer chautauqua presented diverse offerings:

- An hour of love, laughter and song, sponsored by the Methodist Orphanage, Waco.
- Address, 'The Democracy of Religion,' Congressman Luther Johnson, Corsicana, Texas.
- Two 4-minute talks, 'The State Capitol,' and the 'Gardening Industry.'
- Mrs. Emma Boles, home demonstration agent.
- Singing old time songs, led by Walter Amsler, McGregor.
- Entertainment, 'Pigs, Poetry, and Primrose,' by unannounced performers.
- Address, 'Constructive Citizenship,' T. O. Walton, president Agricultural and Mechanical College of Texas.[20]

Neff's active involvement in the Leon River chautauquas attracted a number of his prominent friends and associates: current and future political leaders Tom Connally, Morris Sheppard, and W. Lee O'Daniel, who led his country swing band, The Light Crust Doughboys (and became governor in 1939); the noted Baptist preacher Dr. George W. Truett; and Dr. S. P. Brooks, who served as president of Baylor University for almost three decades. Neff hosted a similar series each summer for many years, later referred to in printed programs as community gatherings or special holiday functions.

Neff also continued sporadic encouragement of D. E. Colp's legislative efforts, which led in 1929 and 1931 to the State Parks Board's contract authority for concession operation of parks. In 1929, Neff returned to active state government as a member of the Railroad Commission, the seeds of interest in state parks planted years earlier on the board's far-flung caravans took hold in several "beauty spots" and other worthy historic sites. By 1932, despite the growing economic depression, Colp edged very close to a deal on prime Palo Duro Canyon land, and he arranged a major concession development for Longhorn Cavern State Park in Burnet County.

That year Neff resigned his Railroad Commission post and accepted the presidency of Baylor University in Waco, a position to rival even the governor's office for someone with Neff's strong Baptist credentials. He graciously accepted Colp's invitation that fall of again "talking parks on the Lord's Day," the Sunday after Thanksgiving, by conducting Longhorn Cavern's opening ceremonies. Although reunited with the state parks movement exactly ten years after he initiated it, Neff couldn't imagine what effect the very recent election of Franklin Roosevelt as President, with Texan John Nance

Garner as his Vice President, would have toward rapid fulfillment of his dream.

Nor could Neff predict that Miriam Ferguson—also recently elected for a return to the Governor's Mansion after a six-year absence—would soon direct huge amounts of federal relief funds for jobs in conservation work. Shortly after her January 1933 inauguration, second-term Governor Ferguson established the Texas Relief Commission—with husband Jim as chairman and Waco businessman Lawrence Whittington Westbrook as director—to channel all federal unemployment-relief dollars toward worthy civic projects. Then in March, soon after Roosevelt's inauguration, the Fergusons and Westbrook learned of a new federal program, the Civilian Conservation Corps (CCC), to recruit young men and assign their labor to conservation projects—including recreation parks.

Westbrook enveloped this Emergency Conservation Work—its official title—in stride, initially controlling both CCC recruitment and assignment of its 200-man camps to specific projects. When President Roosevelt quickly needed help managing the mushrooming national program, he called upon the U.S. Army to transport, pay, feed, clothe, and house CCC recruits in resident camps. And when Governor Ferguson realized her relief commission had little expertise in conservation or state park matters, she telegraphed Pat Morris Neff for guidance in the state's CCC assignments.

> KNOWING YOUR GREAT INTEREST IN AND
> LOVE OF STATE PARKS I THINK THE PUB-
> LIC SERVICE WOULD BE GREATLY BENEFIT-
> TED IF YOU WOULD ACCEPT APPOINT-
> MENT ON THE STATE PARK BOARD STOP
> THE FEDERAL GOVERNMENT IN ALL

PROBABILITY WILL ENDEAVOR TO EX-
TEND STATE PARK PROJECTS MATERIALLY
STOP IN ASKING YOU TO SERVE I HAVE IN
MIND ADDING DIGNITY AND PRESTIGE
TO THE MOVEMENT. . . .

Very close to the tenth anniversary of his creation of the
State Parks Board, Neff now exhibited the personal and govern-
mental credentials for appointment to its membership. "[I]t
would give me great pleasure to serve," he replied, perhaps realizing that his long-pursued dream might now come true, both
for the state, and for Mother Neff Park in particular.

"The world moves slowly," as Neff told the legislature in
1925 concerning the time needed to establish a park system,
"but it moves."[21]

3

Building a Park

By the early 1930s, the elements were in place for an unprecedented state and federal partnership that would eventually elevate the Texas parks system to a new level. While the Texas program and similar efforts by other states had shown signs of success in the previous decade, the promise of even greater opportunities came with the experiment that would be called the Civilian Conservation Corps. And in 1933, when the program debuted at locales across the nation, the American people were more than ready to embrace promise. Eagerness borne of hope was no less evident in Congress, which granted President Roosevelt wide-ranging bipartisan support in his "emergency" conservation-relief effort. Few federal programs have ever faced such anticipation and such scrutiny.

Federal in design and scope and enacted in part through cooperative state efforts, the CCC was at its heart a local program. Its goals and objectives were realized at a multitude of relatively remote sites across the nation. Despite the isolation of the predominantly rural and wilderness projects, word spread quickly to both farm and city that the program seemed to be making a difference. Promise was turning into reality, and at a pace unknown in the depths of the Great Depression.

Perhaps it was the simplicity and universality of the basic CCC concept that fueled most of the stories of early success, since the fieldwork was, by design, labor-intensive and bureaucratically deliberate. Or maybe the good news was the result of the real wages that made a marked difference in the lives of young men and their struggling families. Or, it could have been a product of the human need for the nurturing of change in an era when the status quo offered so much despair and fear. In reality, there was an amalgam of national and personal emotions invested in the CCC, and the dividends were paid out at hundreds of project sites that, in themselves, presaged a new era, one where leisure, historic preservation, conservation, tourism, resource reclamation, and increased federal involvement would become integral elements of the national lifeway.

Civilian Conservation Corps officials used the term "camp" to designate the individual work units of the organization, and that term, in even the broadest of its interpretations, proved to be more than appropriate. Daily life in the CCC camps ranged from the structured discipline of military bivouacs to the social freedom and camaraderie of summer youth gatherings in the country. At times, there was also the "camp" of the vaudeville circuit, as well as that descriptive of a group of people brought together by a common purpose or cause. As the name implied, and certainly as it was understood by CCC officials, these were meant to be temporary installations, although the products of the enrollees' labor was seen as more lasting and perhaps permanent.

President Roosevelt was personally involved in setting up the administrative structure of the CCC, including the decision to place the U. S. Army in the oversight position of field administration. At a White House conference on April 3, 1933, he worked with advisors to draw up an organizational chart for his pet conservation project. Under the initial plan, which remained virtually the same throughout the life of the CCC, the Department of Labor was given the responsibility for criteria used to select enrollees.[1] Although the criteria would change somewhat as the organization evolved, it remained a program for young men from their late teens to their mid-twenties who were from families in need of financial relief. Additionally, the young men had to be U. S. citizens who were unmarried, unemployed, and free of any criminal record. According to CCC literature, they also had to be "In good physical condition and with no history of mental derangement; of good character, with stability of purpose, and a desire for work-experience and self improvement."[2] While some of the requirements might have been somewhat subjective and difficult to prove, other conditions were not. From time to time there were physical criteria, including the retention of at least "three serviceable masticating teeth above and below."[3]

Actual induction of the recruits was the responsibility of the War Department, and its authority soon extended to the administrative structure of camp life, including food, clothing, transportation, and physical conditioning. The selection and supervision of work projects was left to the departments of Interior and Agriculture and their various agencies. As a result, there was a diversity of purpose among the camps that provided some distinction within the organization. Camps were established for specific purposes that focused on programs designed to help ensure the president's goals of land preservation and reclamation. Each program was associated with a particular government bureau. Camp numbers were assigned according to their designation with the organizational structure. Thus, there might be SCS-1 for the Soil Conservation Service, F-3 for the U. S. Forest Service, S-63 for a state forest, and in the case of Mother Neff State Park, SP-38, denoting an association with the State Parks Board through a cooperative effort with the National Park Service. Other CCC programs included range management, reservoir construction, demonstration farms, historic preservation, fire fighting, and wildlife management. Although there was an element of program diversity, the general public perceived only a narrow base of purpose and soon labeled the organization as Roosevelt's "Tree Army" or "Soil Soldiers."[4]

Given the U. S. Army's oversight of field administration, it was not surprising that the camps took on a decidedly military appearance. So strong was the association that many inside and outside the organization believed the CCC actually was, or should be, a military training operation. Officially it was never designed for reserve training, but unofficially, and in retrospect, the military structure certainly prepared young men for the eventuality of service. In that sense, it provided camp commanders as both army regulars and unemployed reservists some limited background in command training and responsibility, albeit in a peacetime setting. It also gave enrollees a taste of military discipline and culture, which many would call upon in the war years that soon followed the CCC experiment.

For administrative purposes, the army divided the nation into nine "corps areas." Texas fell into the eighth, thus the camp numbers in the state identified their area, as in Company 817. Each corps area was headed by a brigadier general or major general. Working down the chain of command to the camp level, the administration included camp commanding officers, normally captains or first lieutenants, and a support staff of second lieutenants, sergeants, and corporals. The U. S. Army established the camps, maintained discipline, ordered supplies, and provided the support necessary to minimize interference with, and thus maximize the efficiency of, work schedules and responsibilities, the domain of the associated bureau.[5]

The basic daily structure of camp life reflected the influence of Old Army. The following schedule from a camp in the Northwest is representative of those established throughout the organization, although there were considerations for local modifications.

6:00 a.m.	Rising bugle
6:15-7:00	Breakfast, followed by sick call
7:15	Police camp and draw tools
7:30	Go to work
11:15	Return from work
12:00	Dinner
1:00	Sick call
1:15	Police camp
1:30	Draw tools
1:45	Go to work
4:45	Return from work
6:00	Supper followed by the study program[6]

Robert L. Nettles, one of the enrollees of Company 817 at Mother Neff, told of the significance of the daily camp inspections:

> We came back [after breakfast] and cleaned our barracks. And you had to clean them, boy. During the day, while we were out working, the officers of the

camp would come around and inspect the cabins, and if they found any dust anywhere—hit your blanket with a quirt, and if any dust came up, you got KP (kitchen patrol) that week, or extra duty. So everything was pretty spotless. . . . You never threw anything down, because you had to pick it up later.[7]

The dress of the day for work projects was generally white cotton tee-shirts, dungarees, and caps, but in the evening the enrollees began looking more like army recruits. After work hours and a shower it was time to put on the "army-type uniforms." As Nettles noted, "In the summertime it was khaki. In the wintertime it was ODs—olive drabs. GI-issue, World War I uniforms of wool." Then, in army fashion, the young men formed in groups by barracks and marched to "retreat," the formal lowering of the colors at the end of the day, before continuing on to supper.[8]

While the army did maintain discipline, its various manifestations were not always in the most serious vein. Camp personnel frequently took advantage of their inherent power and the naiveté of the enrollees to create some light-hearted diversions in the form of pranks. The pranks ranged from the common misguided searches for non-existent tools, such as the left-handed monkey-wrench or a sky hook, to the use of sticky fly-paper applied to exposed posteriors during bogus medical inspections. Although the pranks were most often delivered and received in fun, some did leave lingering impressions. Robert Nettles recalled one in particular that resulted in his new camp moniker. The instigator was the camp's mess sergeant, who had a reputation for a surly and serious demeanor:

When we got through with the noon meal, he come around to me and said, "Go up to the infirmary and

get a bottle of latrine oil." So, I went up to the infirmary to get a bottle of latrine oil. They didn't have
any. They sent me down to the superintendent's office down there, and they didn't have any either. They
sent me to one of the work projects. Everywhere there
was a work project, I went to get this bottle of latrine oil. If I'd been smart, I'd have gone to my barracks and gone to sleep. And so, when the day was
over, it was all over the camp. Everybody knew about
it, and some of the guys started calling me "Latrine
Oil." That was my nickname. They called me that
until I got out of the CCC.[9]

Like the ODs of World War I vintage, housing at the CCC
camps was "GI-issue," in its design if not actual material. Large
wall tents and Sibley tents were used in many instances as temporary housing until more stable forms of construction could
be introduced. Generally, given the temporary mission of the
camps, these were in the form of wooden barracks. Minimalist
in design and function, the barracks were lightly constructed
utilizing either box framing of plank walls or balloon framing
with undersized and overspaced studs. The barracks were built
off the ground for ventilation and to provide a measure of port-
ability. With a relative minimum of effort, the structures could
be placed on trucks or partially dismantled for transportation
to other project locations. They were, in effect, lighter versions
of the shotgun-style and box houses then commonly used in
association with temporary mill and industrial operations across
the nation. The barracks likewise served a temporary function
and were never designed to be a lasting reminder of the CCC
work, although there were unsuccessful efforts at places like
Mother Neff State Park to retain them as tourist cabins. (Most

CCC/World War I barracks held about forty men; Mother Neff, Palmetto, and a handful of other state park operations had the smaller, cottage-like barracks.)

Outside, the barracks were painted or covered with tar paper sheathing. Inside, there was no insulation. A single wood-burning stove might provide the only heat in the winter, but the fires were frequently "turned out" at night for safety reasons, regardless of how cold it got. In the summer, according to Robert Nettles, "it just got hot."[10] There were windows for cross-ventilation, but they were generally small in size and number. Some barracks had partial screening covered by wooden sides that could be propped up in hot weather.

Barracks construction provided space for the mess hall, company offices, educational facilities, the canteen or recreation hall, and living quarters. At Mother Neff, the latter usually contained five or six men in either single or double deck bunk beds. The primary lighting source in all of the structures was electricity, although its use was restricted to early night hours. Generators were turned off shortly after "lights out" each night, again primarily for safety reasons. Electricity was a new luxury for many of the CCC enrollees, most of whom were from agricultural areas where the rural electrification programs of the New Deal era were still years away. Many Texas farms, even those that existed virtually in the shadow of new hydroelectric dams under construction, would not be "hooked up" until the time of World War II. Electricity was a strange convenience, which was not fully appreciated and certainly not understood by many of the young men until later. It eventually moved from curiosity to necessity, as did other conveniences they encountered in camp, including wringer washing machines, refrigeration, and the radio.[11]

While conveniences bordered on luxury for most of the recruits, so did the availability and abundance of food. By all accounts, meals in the CCC were good and bountiful. According to former enrollee Burt Gillis, "As I remember it, I've never eaten better food than I ate in the Civilian Conservation Corps. And I was young then. Boy, I couldn't get enough to eat. Vegetables—always some kind of meat."[12] Robert Nettles agreed: "We always had meat, mostly beef probably. I know we had mashed potatoes, we had beans. For breakfast, we had cereal, maybe, and hotcakes, and just regular breakfast meals." He added, "I weighed approximately 138 then (at enrollment), and about six months later I weighed 150 or more."[13]

Nettles's case was not an exception within the CCC program. Even with hard work and long hours, enrollees generally grew and gained weight on the regimen of regular meals. Although most had come from Texas farms hard hit by floods and then droughts, by devastating erosion and insect invasions, few had known real hunger. Even in the depths of the depression, the largely subsistent farm families managed to raise enough food for meals, although the offerings were often meager and many times lacking in proper amounts of protein and nutrients. In contrast, however, the CCC offered three "squares" a day, with ample amounts of meat, fresh produce, milk, bread, grains, and even deserts. The menus, as well as the cooks, reflected a regional approach to food preparation, and the Southern diet, with its emphasis on animal fats, prevailed at places like Mother Neff. In large part, supplies were purchased from local farmers, and many benefited from the presence of the CCC camps in their area.

Discipline, order, regular meals, shelter, and uniforms were not the only rewards the enrollees enjoyed for their hard work and their enforced separation from family. They generally received a pay equivalent to a dollar a day, or thirty dollars a month. (Some special enrollees who took on additional assignments, such as educational program assistant, could make as much as five or six dollars more a month.) Of that amount, however, at least twenty-five dollars went home to the enrollee's family. This family assistance provision was central to Roosevelt's objective for relief measures. If the young man was an orphan or otherwise without "dependents," the money might remain in an account to be paid out upon discharge from the CCC. The remaining five dollars a month, sometimes paid out in the form of company chits, was the enrollee's "disposable" cash and could be used to buy items at the camp canteen, play songs on the jukebox if there was one, or trade for items in the nearest town. Although the pay seems meager by more recent standards, its impact at the time has to be judged in the context of a worldwide depression. Twenty-five dollars a month was sufficient to make a significant difference for families on relief and without hope of employment in the mid-1930s. As Archie Gibbs told about his family, "It put groceries on the table."[14]

The five dollars enrollees were allowed to keep each month mostly went toward some limited forms of entertainment, and in some cases was enough to get them into trouble in local towns. To paraphrase an old saying, their needs were few and easily met. It was not uncommon, then, for some of the boys to even save part of their monthly stipend. Most of their immediate needs—clothing, food, medical care, linens, toiletry items, and educational materials—were provided by the CCC. In terms of real wages, a 1941 estimate showed, the benefits to the boys were more than twice their paycheck each month.[15]

The work that produced the dollar-a-day wages was strenuous, time-consuming, and labor-intensive. Although the CCC maintained detailed work schedules and project objectives, it was not necessarily in the best interest of the program to accomplish all tasks as quickly as possible. An overarching goal was to keep the young men busy and productive, even if it meant forgoing the efficiency of mechanized equipment for the numbers involved in manual labor. That is not to imply that the camps were without such equipment as earth-movers, tractors, dump trucks, dynamite, and other vestiges of heavy construction; they were not. But, there always remained a constant battle of balance involving the best means to achieve the two primary objectives of the CCC: relief and reclamation. The work projects, while significant, paled in comparison. As park superintendent C. R. Byram noted when he was temporarily transferred from Mother Neff State Park to the CCC project at Daingerfield, in East Texas, where he would help build a lake: "Compared with the REAL construction job of the CCC—that of making men out of boys—a dam is just another pile of dirt."[16]

With organizational structures in place for opening and operating camps, Roosevelt pressed his conservation corps program into action soon after taking office. The first camp, bearing the appropriate name of Camp Roosevelt, opened near Luray, Virginia, in the George Washington National Forest, in April 1933. The following month, officials organized Company 817 at Fort Sill, Oklahoma. The company's first assignment was near Stephenville, Texas, where enrollees built an earthen dam, a road, and a native stone concession building for a short-lived state park (now privately owned). Following that, the boys were temporarily divided into two side camps for work at parks near Mineral Wells and Meridian. The main camp moved to the

Mother Neff site in December 1934, joined later by the group
from Meridian.[17]

The company newspaper, the *Blue Eagle News*, reported
advance notice of the proposed move to the McGregor area in
September 1934:

> This company claims all records for having been
> scheduled to move the most times and places, yet
> never to have moved. The first date set for moving
> was June 10 to the Big Bend Country. Since then
> two more dates have been set to move to the same
> location, followed by a proposed movement to
> Huntsville, later to Brownwood, and we are now
> headed to McGregor or—? Other places not yet
> mentioned are Australia, Hawai [sic], and Devils Is-
> land, or possibly the Virgin Islands.[18]

Other references to the McGregor site followed in subsequent issues of the paper, and then in December, the following poignant, patriotic, and under-punctuated notice appeared:

> When the storm clouds of the depression have
> finally passed from our horizon and we stand no
> longer under the rainbow of hope, but in the actual
> midst of prosperity and the joy of it and the CCC
> has passed into oblivion the boys of the CCC with a
> greater capacity for earning a livelihood, for a place
> in our national social life and with enlarged visions
> will stand radiantly as stalwart citizens in the tri-
> umph of our country as we all together sing the
> psalms of victory. ON TO McGREGOR.[19]

The enrollees' first view of the Neff land was the camp build-ings that would be their home while they worked to develop the park. Again, the newspaper provided an upbeat perspective:

> Even viewed through a drizzling rain, the first impression of the camp layout was pleasing. Cab-ins, mess hall, bath house, infirmary, recreation hall, post exchange, and supply house were a case of "love at first sight." Since scrap lumber, ect. [sic] is being cleaned up and gravel walks are being placed over the entire camp site, the second glimpse proves that the first impression wasn't wrong.[20]

The article does not record the camp building unit, but Neff believed it was a division of the army. More likely, it was con-tracted to local builders, but perhaps under supervision of, or with assistance from, army personnel. Regardless of who built the barracks, it was the army that assumed ownership, and it was that claim that later led to some controversy with Pat Neff at the close of CCC operations in the park.

With the army in overall command of camp administra-tion, it fell to the National Park Service, working in coop-eration with the Texas State Parks Board, to manage the park's development. Central to the cooperative effort was an intri-cate and rigid set of checks and balances that maintained broad concepts of national park planning and architecture, with allowances for an area's natural environment and other regional influences, including history.

The diversified yet distinctive architectural theme of the CCC parks constructed in association with the National Park Service had its roots in popular designs and building styles dat-ing back to the 1880s. Later labeled "NPS Rustic," the architectural theme was, in effect, an amalgam of Frank Lloyd Wright's "organic architecture," the massing and perceived permanence of Romanesque Revival stylings perfected by H. H. Richardson, the order of the Arts and Crafts movement espoused by Gustav Stickley and others, the wilderness grandeur of the Adirondack Great Camps, and the distinctive Bungalow influences of brothers Henry and Charles Greene.[21] While NPS Rustic provided the architectural context for expressing the built environment of the parks in general, it was the reliance on regional adaptability that made each individual set of park buildings a unique collection unto itself. Thus, Mother Neff State Park on the Central Texas Prairies, Palo Duro Canyon along breaks in the High Plains, and Davis Mountains State Park in the rugged hills of West Texas share common recognizable elements of design and interpretation, although they also exhibit dramatic differences in their relationship to their particular surroundings. And, what was true within the state for NPS/CCC parks was true across the nation.

To President Roosevelt, whose own fond memories of the Adirondack camps of his youth in his native state of New York strongly influenced his early interest in the outdoors and in conservation, regionalistic architecture was a primary objective of the New Deal parks programs. The president's deeply held personal concepts of park architecture were not lost on the National Park Service, whose designers and planners took that vision and sought to balance structural form and function with the harmony of natural adaptation. NPS architect Albert H. Good succinctly outlined the program's overarching considerations in the 1935 book, *Park Structures and Facilities*:

> Successfully handled, it is a style which, through the
> use of native materials in proper scale, and through

the avoidance of rigid, straight lines, and over so-phistication, gives the feeling of having been executed by pioneer craftsmen with limited tools. It thus achieved sympathy with natural surroundings and with the past.[22]

Architect Herbert Maier, of the NPS Oklahoma City re-gional office which oversaw projects in Texas and nearby states, further elaborated on the theory behind the style that was cen-tral to park planning in the New Deal:

Since the primary purpose in setting aside semi-wilderness areas is to conserve them in as nearly a primitive state as possible it follows that every struc-ture, no matter how necessary, must be regarded as an intruder and should be designed with an eye to-ward making it inconspicuous. These primitive ar-eas are most beautiful in their native condition, and introducing man-made structures cannot improve the beauty of the whole but tends to rather rob the picture which nature has painted of much of its wholesome effect on the visitor, no matter how pleas-ingly such buildings may have been designed. This may be theory, but it is good theory.[23]

Maier's views were clearly in the mainstream of park phi-losophy at the time, and other NPS architects surely agreed with him when he noted that the word improvement was "an anomaly in dealing with parks." By way of explanation, he added, "Build-ings in parks, like children, are necessary, but if you want your visitors to admire your park buildings or your children, they should be made to keep their place." Echoing the fundamental form-follows-function philosophy of architecture, he also called for a reliance on "architectural accusation," where exterior design accesses, or identifies, the structure's purpose and interior arrangement. He further advocated basic design elements, with little room for the personal tastes and ambitions of project architects. Ultimately, NPS guidelines and an area's natural surroundings were to be the sole arbiters of park design.[24]

NPS rustic, with its obvious organic influences, was ideally suited for natural surroundings, and its primitive nature allowed for discrepancies of craftsmanship and for imperfections of indigenous materials. Cleverly, the style afforded the most stylistic protection for the largely unskilled farm boys of the CCC who learned their professions on the job. That the majority of their major structures have survived with their original design integrity intact for well over a half century and are now praised for their craftsmanship and beauty—and even sometimes listed on the National Register of Historic Places—is a testament to the successful union of architecture and purpose.

To ensure consistency within the framework of regionalism and unskilled labor, and to avoid experimentation outside the parameters of the program, the national Park Service maintained a rigid system of design planning, as well as review and compliance. The agency assigned an architect, architectural historian, and engineer to coordinate the design phase of each park project. Working from a site-specific master plan, drawn up with local input, but finalized by the relevant regional office and by the NPS Branch of Planning in Washington, DC, the design team provided detailed drawing and revisions to the park superintendent, the designated overseer of construction. Providing support throughout the process were representatives of state park authorities, NPS regional offices, camp administration, and, significantly, LEMs (Local Experienced Men). The LEMs, like the families of the young men they supervised and instructed, were largely drawn from the ranks of the unemployed or under-employed. In the development of NPS-CCC parks, they were the seasoned professionals, technical experts, and tradesmen—architects, mechanics, landscape designers, equipment operators, and foremen—who made the final connection between design and labor and between concept and reality.[25]

At the McGregor park site, Herman F. Cason was an early foreman. An architect, Cason first supervised construction of the headquarters building, the concession building, and a blacksmith shop. Additionally, his signature appears on drawings associated with other early buildings in the park. Following his service in the CCC, Cason returned to an architectural practice in Waco and designed a number of commercial, residential, and public buildings. His work included a fire station on Columbus Street and the Elite Cafe, an early roadside landmark on the town's celebrated—some would say infamous—traffic "circle" southeast of the main business district.[26]

Another of the professional leaders at the camp was Walter Kelsey Adams, who served as the camp engineer responsible for survey work. A New York native and a former engineer with the United Fruit Company, Adams received his formal training at Syracuse University and the University of Wisconsin. Following his CCC work, he became an engineer in San Antonio.[27]

Landscape design, central to the success of construction in the former Neff bottomlands, was the responsibility of Stewart E. King, an Austin landscape architect. The Mother Neff park was not the only federal project with which King was associated. He also worked on the Subsistence Homestead Project in Three Rivers, Texas.[28]

One of the most important of the early civilian personnel at Mother Neff was park superintendent C. R. Byram of Belton. Byram proved to be an effective leader, and the detail of his worksite photographs and reports to the National Park Service preserve much of what is known about construction projects in the park. Equally valuable to the historical record are the personal views he included that brought life to the reports and provided insights into the man's motivation and character. In October 1935, for example, he wrote about an awards ceremony recognizing several leadership promotions as well as a number of enrollees who were leaving the company to accept positions as civilian employees with the CCC:

> All of the above mentioned men earned and were given the Park Service Merit Certificate, these Certificates being, in the writers [sic] humble opinion, one of the finest things we get to do for the boys. I like them so well, and think so much of the boys who earn them that I don't mind at all spending about thirty minutes apiece on them, lettering in their names and other data,—that being about the last thing I get to do for them.[29]

In the same report, Byram reacted optimistically, and prematurely it turned out, to reports the CCC might be given permanent status as a federal agency:

> The Presidents [sic] statements relative to the continuation of the CCC as a permanent set-up have caused no end of comment, mostly very favorable. This community is, however, rather "park-minded", having had for a number of years the original Mother Neff Park . . . for use as an assembling place and

recreational center, there being interest to a considerable extent in the work which we are doing.[30]

Byram evidently ran the park efficiently, as his reports to park service personnel show steady progress on the primary construction projects. He was not, however, above a little diversion, especially if it could possibly complement the park's tourism potential. In March 1935, workers were preparing a picnic area in what became known as Indian Cave, or Tonkawa Cave, when they uncovered human remains. Early speculation was that the skeleton was that of an Indian, possibly one of the Tonkawa tribe that roamed the area in historic times. As reported in the *Blue Eagle News*:

> As soon as the first bone was uncovered, Mr. Byram, the park superintendent, was called to the scene, where assisted by Mr. King, landscape architect, the skeleton was slowly unearthed and found to be resting on a flat slab of rock. Intentions at first of the park superintendent were to encase the skeleton in glass and leave it as it lay as a park attraction, but intentions at present are to mount the skull, that has been removed, and place it along with arrowheads, drills, and scrappers [sic] found near the scene in the recreation hall and later move the collection to the concession building that is yet to be built.[31]

Byram excavated another burial at the site the following month. The second skeleton was that of a small child found with an arrowhead in the region of the chest cavity. The paper concluded the presence of the stone weapon was evidence that the burials were more likely of some antiquity, possibly dating to "before the settlement of white men in this neighborhood."[32]

Byram consulted with W. F. Moroney, president of the Central Texas Archeological Society and head of the Sociology Department at Baylor University, and other members of the society regarding the excavations. The ethics of professional archeology being in its formative stages at the time, and thus less sensitive to such issues as the display of human remains, tourism prevailed. The so-called "Tonkawa Indian skulls" were in fact included for a time in a camp museum, along with other local artifacts, both cultural and natural.[33] Later, the remains were reburied and the site was marked with a metal tablet made by members of the CCC. Unfortunately, it failed to provide adequate protection, and looters later stole the skeletons. Only reprinted photographs of the skulls and the CCC newspaper articles remain as evidence of Byram's excavations.

Early in 1935, much of the construction activity at Mother Neff State Park centered around the local quarrying operations that produced the stone for the walls of park structures. Native limestone from several nearby quarry sites along Owl Creek and Horse Creek supplied the rough material. Robert Nettles, who worked on the stonecutting crews, described the process:

> The way they did this, they dug the topsoil off the stone, and they used jackhammers and drilled holes in a pattern and then take what we call "feather and wedges" and a sledgehammer and break these rocks a loose from the mother lode, or whatever you call it. You'd make small rocks from the large rocks and then we'd load them on a stretcher—it was similar to a human stretcher—it had two [long] boards, and boards were nailed across the handles. Two guys could handle that real good. I don't know how much the stones weighed, probably 50 to 100 pounds. And

then they would carry them to a truck and then they'd take them down to where Mother Neff State Park is now and then they had a lot of rock cutters and stonemasons who cut these rocks up into smaller rocks.[34]

The final dressing of the stones took place in the vicinity of the old Neff tabernacle, near the banks of the Leon River.

The dangerous nature of such work, coupled with the young men's inexperience in heavy construction, made safety a primary concern at the Mother Neff camp. Enrollees were supervised closely, and precautionary rules were followed in actual practice as well as in regular safety drills. Regardless, there were accidents, but most, including poisonous snake and insect bites, were of the type that could be treated at the infirmary. Unfortunately, however, there were deaths at the camp. The first occurred in July 1935, when Virgil Chaney, a 21-year-old enrollee from Bluff Dale, in Erath County, was struck by lightning. Chaney had just completed his work assignment for the day and was returning to camp with his shovel over his shoulder when he was hit. Stephenville enrollee Herman Baker was injured by the same lightning strike, but returned to the project after a brief hospital stay.[35]

The death of Virgil Chaney had a profound impact on the other enrollees who, like most young people, are not aware of their own mortality and vulnerability until they have to face the reality. The tragic accident influenced a fellow worker, Beryl Kay, to write a commemorative poem for the *Blue Eagle News*:

Gone to Rest

There is an empty space in our midst,
Of a friend that has gone to rest;
He proved himself to be a man
In every given test.

His flashing smile now is gone,
But his ready laughter will stay,
And the memory lingers on
Until that Judgement Day.

He was taken from us by a hand,
Much stronger than the hand of man,
Laughing one minute, gone the next,
To a strange and wonderous land.

But we know that we shall see him,
When our stay on earth is done;
He will stand at the gate and greet us,
When we make that trip alone.

And try to live a better life,
As our friend would have us do.
As he proved himself a man,
Let's prove ourselves one too.[36]

The second death at the camp occurred in late May 1938, shortly before the camp closing. Enrollee Robert G. Howard was killed and several others were injured when a camp truck overturned on its way back from a quarry site.[37]

By the end of 1935, most of the park's major early building, trail, and road projects were under construction. But, despite the superintendent's glowing reports and the positive articles in the camp newspaper, work was not going fast enough for its unofficial overseer, Pat Neff. In October, he drafted a lengthy and sarcastic letter to national and state park leaders describing in detail his personal agenda for the property. His words left no doubt about his frustration, revealing his preference for product over planning and his lack of respect for the "laboring mountain" of bureaucracy. It is also clear what he thought of NPS Rustic and its promoters. Addressing first one of the central buildings, the clubhouse(concession building), he observed:

> For nearly a year the clubhouse at Mother Neff Park has been discussed, planned, considered, and proposed from Washington to Austin. Architects, landscape experts, and contractors have all had it under consideration. After the passing of these many months, the laboring mountain has brought forth a mass—a wonderful clubhouse. It actually consists of two water toilets and a cold drink stand separated by a large open hallway marked 'pavilion.' This hallway is a big open hallway exactly the same kind of building as one on my farm in which to place hay and the farm implements. All that can be said in behalf of it is that it has a roof over it supported by some cedar posts.
>
> To add to the absurdity of it, a fire-place has been added to this hallway. Anybody who has spent one day during the wintertime in Texas would know that this fire-place was an absurdity. It cannot serve as a thing of beauty and certainly not as a thing of

utility. If a norther was blowing, which produces cold weather in Texas, no one would dare occupy this wonderful structure. No one would be foolish enough to build a fire in it because it could not possibly be of any service to anyone in the world. . . . I do not see that this clubhouse could be of any service whatever to the park. It should be named what the major part of the building was built for and marked 'For Men Only.' [38]

Neff also took the architects to task for their lack of planning with regard to a main entrance. Apparently envisioning something along the lines of a grand entry or gateway, he wrote:

Originally it was planned that we should have a magnificent entry into this park. With this in view, acting on the suggestions of the high-powered architects and blue-printers, an additional tract of land, a rugged knoll, was secured and added to the park in order that a befitting entrance should be made. Rocks were brought from the quarry to the entrance, and for some six months work was extended in order to establish this entrance to the park. It has now been determined, so I was advised yesterday, that the entrance site has now been abandoned and that there will be no entrance to the park except an open space. In other words, the wire gap will be let down so the people can drive in.[39]

It is unclear from Neff's remarks where the entryway was originally planned, but his reference to the additional knoll property relates to a narrow strip of land along the present highway. Apparently, the idea was to enter at the top of the hill leading to the park, near where the superintendent's home is now located. Eventually, he got his grand entryway, but it was built in the lower part of the park near the central buildings as one of the last construction projects.

Neff continued his lengthy letter, attacking decisions related to the observation tower/water tank project, the sewer system, and the landscape. He concluded his remarks with clear frustration, revealing both xenophobia and personal disdain for the work and clearly implying that ultimately his guiding hand would shape the park in the image he perceived:

> I can scarcely believe that those to whom this letter has been dictated are responsible for the slow work and for the measley plans finally adopted in connection with the improving of this park. I rather think that someone who has never been to Texas and has never seen the park and knows but little about the affairs of the State has had final say in regard to the work in this particular park. . . .
>
> I am not at all discouraged, however, in reference to this park. It is going to be made a real park. It is going to be the center of religious, educational, and cultural refinement in Central Texas. Later it will have a clubhouse built in the park with these toilets in the back yard to serve their purpose. I am not even hoping that any changes in the clubhouse can be made, for this clubhouse as it is now stands is the result of much labor, much correspondence, much visiting, and the expenditure of much money, and before a change could be made, I am sure that somebody some bright morning would order the camp removed. So we will take it just as it is and get the best results possible out of it.[40]

Neff provided no elaboration of the term "we," but it is thought it was a very small and select group—perhaps no larger than one.

Pat Neff may have been unhappy with circumstances in 1935, but he was not in charge, and work continued on the implementation of the master plan as approved in Washington, Oklahoma City, and Austin. CCC crews blasted rock from the scenic route while others began work on the combination water tower and observation deck. A special tram rail line utilizing a small engine known to the campers as the "P.U.T" (Poosh-em Up Tony) moved large, "six-man" rocks to the tower site at a promontory on the upper east side of the park. Late in January 1936, Superintendent Byram reported to the NPS that the observation tower was complete except for the iron railing.[41]

Work on the concession building, a central feature of the lower park, also began in 1935. Prior to the initial foundation work, however, landscape crews used heavy equipment as well as shovel brigades to build a six-foot-high terrace at the building site. Viewed today, the elevation change is barely noticeable, but the magnitude of the undertaking at the time attracted numerous visitors from nearby towns. The purpose of the terracing was to allow the building to remain above the known flood stage of the Leon River, even though it would eventually include a basement, and to cover an intricate stone-lined culvert system that ran between a slough in the picnic area and the river's edge. The concession building was originally designed to serve as a refectory, to provide "canteen" and dance floor space, and to provide housing for a caretaker.[42]

By the summer of 1936, other construction projects included culverts and rock bridges along the scenic route. Plans were also underway to reroute the main road through the park so the

Public Works Administration could construct a new bridge across the Leon at the edge of the park boundary. Here Neff once again used his political muscle. Working directly with the Texas Highway Department, most notably state highway engineer Gibb Gilchrist, he managed to bring about the new route, which eventually opened the old roadbed inside the park for construction of a large pavilion. Neff, in his normal self-effacing but politically direct manner, had urged Gilchrist to support the project for the common good, and not because of Neff's personal interest. In a reply to that suggestion, Gilchrist wrote:

> I am glad that what you say is true, that while this matter is intensely personal to you, that it is also of great public interest. I am glad to say that you are as free from letting personal interest mix with public interest as any man I know, and as you may surmise, I know some mighty good people.[43]

Gilchrist's response reflects his clear understanding of politics, especially the kind practiced by men like Neff in the 1930s.

With plans for the new bridge approved, CCC officials were free to develop plans for the new building. In November 1936, the Blue Eagle News reported architect Guy Newhall, who replaced Herman Cason at the camp, and engineer W. K. Adams were drawing plans for what would be a large, open-sided pavilion, a new centerpiece for the lower park. Newhall was an important addition to the design team. A native of Maine educated at Trinity University in Hartford, Connecticut, and at the Parsons School of Fine and Applied Arts in New York, he brought skills in both architecture and interior design to his CCC work. Following his service at Mother Neff, Newhall would gain respect for his continued architectural work with firms in both Corpus Christi and San Antonio.[44]

Newhall and Adams worked on the pavilion plans during the remainder of 1936 and submitted them to the Oklahoma City office for approval early in 1937, but a response from the regional landscape architect, H. H. Cornell, clearly showed his concern for building on a flood-prone terrace:

> The project application states that 'the known high water mark' is 616.0. We assume that at frequent intervals flood stage may go beyond this point. The building plans indicate the stage floor at 619.5. On the proposed site, to meet these grades, 25,000 yards of fill will be necessary. Even with this amount of fill, the building will give the appearance of standing upon an abrupt knoll.[45]

Concern over the positioning of the proposed pavilion reflected the differences that often existed between park planners of the National Park Service and officials of the State Parks Board. Their perspectives and objectives were often at odds. In a follow-up letter to William J. Lawson, executive secretary of the Texas State Parks Board, NPS Regional Officer Herbert Maier tried to remove his office from any future blame for the decision to build in the flood plain:

> Since undoubtedly the Leon River will from time to time rise at Mother Neff State Park to a height which will be above the floor level of the recreational pavilion at the park, we feel that this situation should be faced frankly so that no criticism will later be made as to the policy of erecting a building under such conditions. Of course we all know that water may

not rise to such a level more than on an average of
once in twenty years, and the foundations have been
so designed and the masonry walls and masonry floor
will be so constructed that an acute rise in the river
will not seriously damage the building.

Will you please write a letter to my office, expressing an understanding of this situation, and that
in spite of this condition the Texas State Parks Board
desires that the recreational pavilion be placed at the
site selected?[46]

Maier's warning would prove to be prophetic, especially after
the 1954 construction of Lake Belton downstream on the Leon
River. In 1992, when the dam backed up water into the Neff
bottomlands, the level rose to almost 635 feet, over fifteen feet
higher than the 619.5 feet that was cause for concern in 1937.
For months at the height of the flood, only about two feet of
the tabernacle's gabled roof showed above the water as motor-
boats occasionally powered by.[47]

At the end of 1937, another controversy emerged—one to
which Neff once again lent his guiding hand and his outspoken
nature. The new center of his attention was the caretaker's house
(later the superintendent's home), which he felt was inadequate
for his vision of the park as a center of significant events and
tourism. Neff's correspondence from the summer of 1937 included the following note to NPS regional officer Herbert Maier:

I was in Austin a few days ago and a new blue
print was being made of the contemplated caretaker's house at Mother Neff Park. Some three
months ago, I had approved a blue print of this building which was practically a duplication of the care-

taker's house at Cleburne Park. . . . It is true that building materials have advanced in price during the past year but I am wondering if we can't strain a point and have a building in the Mother Neff Park as originally planned.[48]

Neff's frustration came from continued debate among park designers about the function of the caretaker's residence. Initial discussions had included an additional lodge for guest quarters. Budgetary considerations, however, had narrowed the scope and combined the two structures into one, leaving only one room, a bath, and a single garage slot which William J. Lawson described as, "lodge accommodations for distinguished visitors and other people who appear officially before the people in this park."[49]

Objecting to continued efforts by the NPS to downsize the project for economic reasons, Lawson added:

We think this would be an inopportune time to raise the question about the cost of caretakers dwellings in Texas. At the time the present administration of the Texas State Parks Board came into office it found such caretakers dwellings as those at Cleburne, Bastrop and Lockhart. All of these cost much more money and mandays than this proposed caretakers dwelling which we are submitting for Mother Neff SP No. 38. . . .[50]

Given the modest size of the caretaker's house as it was initially built, the discussion of the minimal additional space seems overblown. But traditionally, homes for the resident personnel at parks were quite small, and little consideration was given to future needs or modernization.

Toward the end of 1937, the *Blue Eagle News* was reporting elements of significant change for CCC crews at Mother Neff State Park. The last of the major projects—the caretaker's house, the pavilion, and the stone gateway—were nearing completion or in the final stages of design review. Earlier rumors of severe cutbacks in the CCC program had become a reality, and eighty enrollees were forced to leave Company 817 as part of the downsizing. Plans for a new highway to the park, a route that would become known as the Old River Road, were underway. And, as the paper reported on July 25, 1937, there were mounting concerns about instability abroad:

> There are rumors of political tension in both Japan
> and Europe.
>
> And for Europe—The situation over there is some
> what delicate—Recently the Spanish Loyalists started
> a great offensive in Madrid—the Japanese are or-
> dering the Chinese off their own territory—Yes
> 'umm it is some delicate—Au Revoir—[51]

Robert Nettles, who joined Company 817 late in 1937, was among the last of the CCC boys to leave the camp at Mother Neff the following year. Before his transfer to the camp at Brownwood, where he would help build another state park, he was assigned to one of the final work details:

> They did some things back then that I didn't think
> was right. We had all these uniforms that they had
> in the supply house, and they took them out and
> burned them (near the mess hall). In our recreation
> hall they had a piano, and we were supposed to take
> it out to the dump ground. Well, we took it out to

the dump ground all right, but we loaded it on one of the state men's pickup trucks and he took it home.[52]

Although Neff would win a reprieve of sorts, securing an agreement to have a side camp from Cleburne State Park finish some of the landscaping and trails at Mother Neff, the work of the CCC was completed by the end of June. Describing his visit to the park at that time, Neff wrote to Lawson: "It had the sad atmosphere of the closing of school. By 5 o'clock in the afternoon the camp was another 'deserted village.'"[53]

July 1, 1938, marked the official end of the work details at Mother Neff for the young men of CCC Company 817. Their time in the park had been productive, lasting, strenuous, taxing, and even life-threatening at times, but they had accomplished their tasks diligently through a dual administrative system of military review and civilian training. Memories of work in the CCC camps left the enrollees with mixed emotions, and perhaps Bill Denton spoke for more than himself when he reflected: "I wouldn't take a million dollars for what I went through, and I wouldn't give you a dime to go back through it again."[54]

The completion of the construction phase at Mother Neff State Park brought an end to the most visible aspect of CCC life. Gone was the ordered alignment of the camp on the hill. Gone also was the sight of work crews of young men headed to local quarries in the camp truck, or freshly scrubbed enrollees in their vintage ODs walking the streets of McGregor and Moody. The visible aspect of CCC development at Mother Neff occurred essentially between 1934 and 1938. During that time, however, there was another form of development taking place, one which Superintendent Byram surely realized made the constructed vestiges of the CCC pale in comparison.

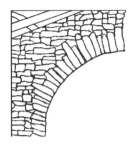

4

Camp Life

As historian John A. Salmond noted in his seminal history of the Civilian Conservation Corps, President Franklin Roosevelt saw the program as a catalyst for bringing together "two wasted resources, the young men and the land, in an attempt to save both."[1] Thus, at Mother Neff, as the task of repairing and preparing the land for a new state park went forward, so too did the reconstruction of the enrollees' lives—financially, physically, and mentally. In the personal equation of the CCC, brawn, labor, and nutrition were balanced by education and the development of character and social skills.

The venue for individual improvement was camp life, where countless opportunities for education were presented daily. Many came through the work assignments, and enrollees learned such lifetime skills as masonry, construction, metalwork, landscaping, surveying, and mechanical repair. More important, perhaps, was their exposure to teamwork, discipline, authority, and social interaction. These social skills were a part of life after work as well, and enrollees moved in differing paces toward maturity in an environment far removed from their homes, where a random group of people would become, at least temporarily, their friends, family, and community. This is why, to a large degree, most former enrollees recall their camp time with fondness and view the experience as a period of positive growth and development. It is also a reason why talk of the so-called "good times" is an integral part of CCC alumni gatherings and reunions across the nation, including those at Mother Neff State Park.

Education, at least in its formal, academic sense, was not initially a program priority within the CCC, and director Robert Fechner long considered it secondary to the national objectives of relief and conservation. As a result, educational programs in the CCC at first suffered from a national lack of focus, and inconsistencies in curriculum, materials, and teacher training were common. Adding to the problem was the army's initial opposition to a centralized plan, perhaps fueled by its fear of losing control or by a mistrust of what it might have considered to be liberal educators and social experimenters. The army's position was reflected in the personal statement of Col. Duncan Major, a War Department representative to the CCC's Advisory Council, in his reaction to a rumor that the president would use the program to provide jobs for unemployed teachers:

> I have constantly fought the attempts of long-haired
> men and short-haired women to get in our camps .
> . . we are going to be hounded to death by all sorts
> of educators. Instead of teaching the boys how to do
> an honest day's work we are going to be forced to
> accede to the wishes of the long-haired men and
> short-haired women and spend most of the time on
> some kind of an educational course.[2]

Despite such opposition, the army soon found itself in an indefensible position and eventually bowed to pressures—public, private, and political—and assumed a leadership position with regard to camp educational programs. As expected, such reversals in philosophy and focus did not come easily or quickly, and there continued to be inconsistencies that held back progress throughout the life of the CCC. As a result, the early successes came largely through local efforts and through the personal action of company commanders. It was at the camp level that programs were the most progressive, meaningful, and efficient.

Given the longtime association between the planned park in Coryell County and Baylor University, especially through Pat Neff, who had been named president of the Waco institution in 1932, it was not surprising that Camp SP-38 would be among those with a strong program. Neff's commitment to education was long-standing. First appointed to the governing board of Baylor University in 1903, he had also, as governor, signed legislation creating Texas Technological College (later Texas Tech University) and South Texas State Teachers College (now Texas A&M University at Kingsville).[3] Years earlier, he had initiated the successful summer chautauquas—centered on educational programs—at the family park site and provided the motivational signs bearing pithy and inspirational phrases that dotted its landscape during his ownership.

An association with Neff meant an association with Baylor, and the ex-governor used his college presidency in a personal way to support the CCC's work on the family's former lands. In a monthly report to the National Park Service in 1935, superintendent C. R. Byram noted: "Through the efforts of former Governor Neff, who is thoroughly and sincerely behind this camp in all it's [sic] activities, very reduced rates have been ob-

tained for members of this camp to all football games in which
Baylor University participates."[4] More importantly, Neff provided special scholarships for CCC enrollees who might choose
Baylor for higher education work. Burt Gillis was one of those
who benefited from the program, but, as he recalled, overall it
was a short-lived experiment primarily because the dropout rate
proved to be relatively high among the CCC enrollees.[5]

Regardless of the educational offerings of the camps, they
could not be confused with the curricula of preparatory schools,
and the student body in the camps were frequently in greater
need of remedial assistance than college courses. Neff nonetheless made sure there was contact between the faculty, the students, and the young men of the CCC. He was, after all, molded
in the patriarchal order of the Victorian era, and both the camp
and the college were part of his extended family. Neff was also
not above using, or at least enjoying, the "common touch" as a
means of publicity. An article in the Corpus Christi Times in
1937, apparently a press release, was entitled "CCC Garden at
Neff Park Planted by College Head." It noted:

> [Neff] never fails to take at least one helping of beans
> when he dines with officials of Company 817. To
> make sure there would be plenty of "cherries" in the
> company garden this year he came [to the McGregor
> camp] recently in work clothes and planted the bean
> rows himself.[6]

The effectiveness of the CCC's educational programs, even
with local support and a strong collegiate association, was miti-
gated to a large extent by the fact that the courses were not
compulsory. They also proved to be somewhat perfunctory, de-
void of the accepted standardization, evaluation tools, adminis-

trative review, and accountability that local school trustees had
come to expect in their respective districts. Critics of the CCC's
educational programs, including Representative Albert Thomas,
a Texas Democrat from Houston, openly questioned the valid-
ity of on-the-job training, as opposed to academic classes. Thomas wanted more lasting results, and he argued that permanent, agency status for the CCC would result in stronger academic direction. His arguments for improvements on both
counts ultimately failed.[7]

While the national debates played out between political
maneuverings and administrative promises and between professional educators and army directors, the reality of educational
programs within the camps often fell far short of even the most
conservative goals. At the Mother Neff camp, enrollees were
offered much, but chose relatively little. Courses included typ-
ing, engineering computation, business arithmetic, electrical
wiring, English composition, and metal arts, and there was even
a camp orchestra. Additionally, there was instruction in diesel
mechanics taught for a time in the shops of the McGregor
Chevrolet Company.[8]

By 1935, the camp boasted an educational advisor, one of
the program's LEMs, and an enrollee staff of one or two who
were paid extra for their assistance. The first advisor noted in
the camp newspaper was R. H. Williams, a graduate of Simmons
College (later Hardin-Simmons University) at Abilene. Williams had a varied career prior to his CCC service. He worked as
a reporter in Dallas and later studied English at Harvard before
teaching stints at Northeastern College in Boston and with the
Uvalde public school system. Williams utilized his enrollee as-
sistants to maintain records and to check books out of the camp
library. For teachers, he had to rely on volunteers, and possibly

some moonlighting instructors, from nearby towns. As the program progressed, more paid instructors were added.[9]

Under Williams's direction, Company 817 offered twenty-nine classes in the spring of 1935. Of those, five were for elementary-level skills, five were regular high school subjects, thirteen were vocational in nature, one was a college course, and five were listed as "general." The most popular course that semester was a dance class with an enrollment of fifty-five. According to the *Blue Eagle News*, "L. R. Hill's dancing class, aided by Ronald Wells at the piano" enjoyed regular and perfect attendance. Following close in interest were auto mechanics and physical education classes, each with fifty-three students. Next in popularity, but with less than half the enrollment, were offerings in etiquette, cooking, and business math. Clearly, courses in the social graces rivaled those designed to teach business skills and trades, which speaks to priorities the young men had established.[10]

The educational classes, like the camp itself, were segregated. While there were a small number of African-American enrollees, all of whom worked on kitchen detail, they were housed in separate areas. Their educational opportunities were also separate, and far from equal, as the Blue Eagle News noted in 1935:

> The six colored enrollees will carry on a school of their own in their cabin, with Willie Summers, a high school graduate, in charge. They began Thursday afternoon after KP duty, three of them studying general elementary subjects. The other three, including the teacher, will take up typing.[11]

Any discussion of the educational aspects of the CCC would be incomplete without some mention of those ancillary programs

Pat Neff at the entrance to the rockshelter that became known as Tonkawa Cave after Indian remains were uncovered by CCC workers. *Courtesy of The Texas Collection, Baylor University*

This early photo of the pavilion shows the flanking pergolas which were later destroyed by floods. The original horizontal design, coupled with the large central archway, architecturally reflects the limestone ledges and rockshelters found in the area. *Courtesy of The Texas Collection, Baylor University*

Pat Neff astride one of his prized stock animals, which he allowed to roam loose in the park. When the presence of the livestock became a nuisance for campers, park officials required Neff to restrict their range to the upper reaches of the park. *Courtesy of The Texas Collection, Baylor University*

An early photo of the observation tower built by the CCC atop a high promontory near the superintendent's house. The structure's rock veneer provides a rustic natural cover for a water storage tank. *Courtesy of The Texas Collection, Baylor University*

An aerial view of the CCC camp taken during the special Mother's Day celebration, May 12, 1935, shows the ordered symmetry of the military-type barracks around a central mott of trees. Visible to the left (north) are baseball and football fields. Cars can be seen along the main road that became State Highway 236. In the distance are farms and buildings associated with Whitson, a dispersed community of the 1930s. The present park entrance, not shown, is several hundred yards to the south (right). *Courtesy of The Texas Collection, Baylor University*

Details of the CCC camp at Mother Neff Park can be seen in this aerial photo taken during Mother's Day festivities, May 12, 1935. Visitors gather for a ceremony in front of the camp at the symbolic lone star feature (right center). Note the lines of uniformed CCC enrollees. *Courtesy of The Texas Collection, Baylor University*

CCC workers constructed this rustic-style picnic table unit adjacent to a large shade tree. In the background is one of the small cabins that was possibly constructed with the assistance of the National Youth Administration. The cabins were used through the war years, but eventually phased out and either dismantled or relocated off park property. *Courtesy of The Texas Collection, Baylor University*

This early photo of the Clubhouse (Concession Building) shows the horizontal nature and rustic detail of the National Park Service design. The central breezeway includes the large stone fireplace Pat Neff found objectionable. *Courtesy of The Texas Collection, Baylor University*

Pat Neff was remembered by friends, colleagues, and Baylor students, in part, for his sartorial neatness, which clearly shows in this photo. Note the starched collar, a trademark of his wardrobe even years after its popularity had waned in general fashion circles. *Courtesy of The Texas Collection, Baylor University*

This photo from the interior of Tonkawa Cave shows the "natural" landscaping of steps fashioned by the Civilian Conservation Corps. Original park plans called for the cave to be utilized as a picnic area, with table and cooking units, but facilities were later removed in favor of the site's natural setting. *Courtesy of Dan K. Utley*

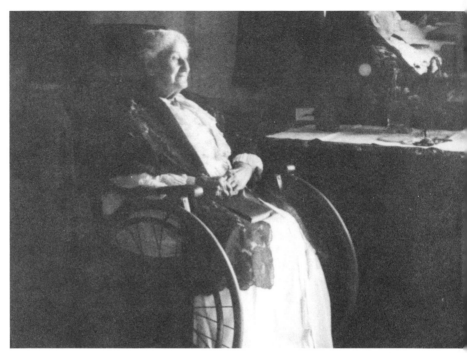

This poignant portrait captures the likeness of Isabella Shepherd Neff in her later years. According to the story often told by her son, Pat M. Neff, she was the inspiration for his establishment of the state park system. Mother Neff State Park, developed on family land, is named in her honor. *Courtesy of The Texas Collection, Baylor University*

Few visitors to Mother Neff State Park realize the extent of the landscaping projects undertaken by the Civilian Conservation Corps. This culvert, one of numerous drainage features in the park, shows how planners utilized rustic styling even in utilitarian areas not designed to be seen by the general public. *Courtesy of Dan K. Utley*

Even when cultural landscape features are clearly evident, as with these hillside steps on the hiking trail system, site preparation, including contouring, boulder placement, and vegetation plantings, often goes unnoticed. Such "invisible" work is a testament to the careful planning of NPS officials and to the landscaping craftsmanship of the CCC. *Courtesy of Dan K. Utley*

Visitors to Mother Neff State Park via State Highway 236 enter through battered pylons and adjacent low walls built by the CCC as one of the last projects in the park. Company 817 moved out before the entryway was completed, and a side camp from Cleburne State Park was brought in to finish the work. *Courtesy of Dan K. Utley*

This detail of a pavilion arch shows the level of quality characteristic of NPS Rustic architecture and CCC craftsmanship. Despite decades of exposure to the elements, precise alignments, differing finish textures, and tight joints still convey the subtle beauty, simplicity, and stability of the styling. *Courtesy of Dan K. Utley*

This wall sconce on the clubhouse shows the intricate beauty of the metalwork crafted by the young men of the CCC. Additional metalwork of note, including lighting fixtures, hinges, and rafter joinery, remain integral architectural elements within the park. The metal craftsmanship of Company 817 was prominently featured in a special CCC exhibit at the 1936 Texas Centennial at Dallas. *Courtesy of Dan K. Utley*

This wintertime scene of the Old River Road shows the meandering alignment representative of the Leon River which flows nearby. Recently the subject of intense public debate over the continued preservation of its historical integrity, the road was originally constructed as a result of federal funds and the political clout of Pat M. Neff. As the park it served, it is now listed on the National Register of Historic Places. *Courtesy of Dan K. Utley*

Detail of the stonework in the refectory (concession building) breezeway. Note the large fireplace, which Pat Neff criticized as being useless in such an open area, and the lone star design in the floor. *Courtesy of James W. Steely*

This view from inside the refectory breezeway, looking south to the pavilion, shows the intricate detail of stonework, roof trusses, and a metal chandelier. To the left of the fireplace is an original chair constructed by CCC enrollees. *Courtesy of James W. Steely*

Evidence of the scale of CCC work can be seen in this construction photo of the pavilion, with its massive stone and frame arbor arcade, timbered roof trusses, and terraced building site, elevated several feet above the existing Leon River floodplain by enrollee labor. *Courtesy of National Archives, National Park Service files*

This Goldbeck panorama shot shows CCC Company 817 as it appeared in 1935. *Courtesy of Mother Neff State Park*

An early photo of the superintendent's home, which Pat Neff fought to enlarge, in part to accommodate "visiting dignitaries." *Courtesy of Charlotte Wright Weiss*

Cabins from the National Youth Administration camp at Mother Neff Park, ca. 1940. The photo indicates the camp was on the upper reaches of the park, in the vicinity of the earlier CCC camp facilities. Note the electric lines, stovepipes, and the side panels that were propped open to provide shade for screened windows. *Courtesy of Mother Neff State Park, courtesty Jack G. White*

Interior view of the CCC recreation building, ca. mid-1930s. Note the small cor-
doned area to the right rear that served as the office space for the camp newspaper, the
Blue Eagle News. Courtesy of Mother Neff State Park, courtesy Mrs. Harry Blackburn

The ca. 1940 NYA recreation building, still extant on park property, later served as a
church building. *Courtesy of Mother Neff State Park, courtesy Charlotte Wright Weiss*

CCC enrollee Harry Britton proudly stands beside the camp's new truck. Although the organization often inherited military surplus materials, there were occasionally new pieces of equipment. Many enrollees learned the basics of engine mechanics by working on camp vehicles. Note the Magnolia Company license plate brackets, most likely not GI issue. *Mother Neff State Park, courtesy Mrs. Harry Blackburn*

CCC enrollees at the Mother Neff camp in their standard issue dungarees, or work clothes. Their official wardrobe also included military-style uniforms, known as ODs for their olive drab color, which were reserved for evening functions and special occasions. *Mother Neff State Park, courtesy Mrs. Harry Blackburn*

Harry Blackburn (left) and an unidentified fellow enrollee at work on a native stone feature within the park. Masonry and construction techniques were some of the fundamental trade skills taught to many of the CCC boys. *Mother Neff State Park, courtesy Mrs. Harry Blackburn*

Local resident Mary Lavauhn Ritchie, age five, posed for this picture at the gateway to the Neff family park. The inscription on the arch was typical of the inspirational statements Pat Neff placed throughout the park during his family's ownership. *Mother Neff State Park, courtesy Mary Ritchie Wright*

Former members of CCC Company 817 gathered for an anniversary reunion at the park in 1984. The "boys" are pictured in front of the entry arch of the pavilion many of them constructed almost a half century earlier. *Courtesy of Texas Parks and Wildlife Department*

The "museum" area in the refectory breezeway included displays on the natural and cultural history of Texas, as well as the park environs. Note the mounted ram head, Indian artifacts, and park furniture. The Sam Houston portrait to the right of the chimney was lost in the 1992 flood; a duplicate copy has since been donated to the park archives. *Courtesy of The Texas Collection, Baylor University*

Picnic facilities in the area of the old reunion grounds at Mother Neff State Park. Visible in the background are cabins left over from the NYA camp. *Courtesy of The Texas Collection, Baylor University*

The original horizontal line configuration of the wooden roof shingles can be seen in this early photo of the refectory. *Courtesy of The Texas Collection, Baylor University*

An early community gathering in the park pavilion. Note the chandeliers, elevated stage area, and the CCC-crafted wooden pews. *Courtesy of The Texas Collection, Baylor University*

Superintendent Pete Carpenter surveys the devastating floodwaters by boat in 1992. *Courtesy of Steven D. Reece, Waco Tribune-Herald*

Actor David Jones, portraying Gov. Pat M. Neff, speaks with Gov. George W. Bush following a Capitol ceremony commemorating the 75th anniversary of the Texas state parks system. The ceremony included a dramatization of Neff's efforts on behalf of state parks and his signing of the bill creating the State Parks Board in 1923. *Courtesy of Texas Parks & Wildlife Department.*

that helped to support the general objectives. At the Mother Neff camp, the two most successful examples were the library and the company newspaper. The camp library was part of a general CCC policy that attempted to offer enrollees access to good books, training materials, the literature of the day, and popular periodicals. As with the broad educational policies of the CCC, however, the differences between program objectives and the reality of practice within the camps was often significant. Corps literature regarding the setup of camp libraries, understandably idealistic in tone and scope, called for detailed planning, organization, and even standardized floorplans. In many instances, such as at the Mother Neff camp, the library was a designated area within the recreation hall. A description of the building's redesigned and rehabilitated interior in 1935 reveals the elements that competed for the enrollees' leisure time:

> We ask you to observe the stained walls, burnt ceiling, glass encased library, rugs, curtaining, easy chairs, divans, bridge sets, smoking acomodations [sic], ping pong table, and general arrangement.
> With popular tunes coming from the hall piano, one certainly has the feeling of being in a home.[12]

The "glass encased library" was most likely a set of barrister bookcases. If they were stocked according to CCC recommendations, they might have included books on forestry, agriculture, history, trades, sports, nature, businesses, and travel, as well as works of fiction. Recommended magazines included *School Life, Time, Home Craftsman, Popular Mechanics, Popular Science, Readers' Digest,* and *National Geographic.*[13] In the ideal situation, the camp library would complement the camp's educational programs, but in many cases they were merely small collections of donated books and magazines. In an effort to improve the library's function at Mother Neff, the camp eventually affiliated as a branch of the McLennan County library system in order to offer a wider range of materials.[14]

One of the most widely read forms of literature within the CCC companies was the camp newspaper. Written and printed by enrollees, it was an integral part of the program, providing news closely related to camp activities. The camp newspaper represented, in most instances, variations on school newspapers, with stories about upcoming events in entertainment and sports, reports on work assignments, and camp gossip. Very little was included about state or national events; the newspapers offered light reading that promoted camaraderie and positive attitudes. Given their oversight by camp administrators, there was no room for dissent or for discouraging pieces.

Camp newspapers were common in the CCC, and most camps of lasting duration had one. Their titles frequently reflected the company's purpose, the camp name, the geographical and environmental setting, or local and national history. In Texas, for example, camp newspapers included the *Apple Corps News* at Apple Springs, the *Cactus* at Mathis, *Camp Leonard Wood News* in Woodville, the *Barrage* in Goliad, the *Duster* in Hereford, the *Kamp Kleberg Klatter* in Floresville, the *Mill Whistle* in Groveton, the *Windy Rim* in Canyon, and the *Mosquito* in Karnack. There were also work-related titles, such as the *Pick and Shovel* in Temple, the *Eight Hours a Day* in Livingston, and the *Gold Brick* in Jasper. Additionally, there were titles whose meanings were not as easily discerned, including the *Buccaneer* in Taylor or the *Bloodhound* in Sherman.[15]

At the Mother Neff camp, the newspaper was the *Blue Eagle News*, a title derived from the ubiquitous symbol of Roosevelt's

National Recovery Administration (NRA). The NRA was a controversial and short-lived New Deal agency designed to provide a system of industrial codes to aid recovery, and participating businesses displayed signs bearing a blue eagle and the phrase "We Do Our Part." To many, the blue eagle became an important symbol of patriotism and of cooperation with government policies. Not everyone saw it that way, however, and eventually the NRA was declared unconstitutional as an infringement on interstate commerce. As a result, the *Blue Eagle News*, which was published until the end of the McGregor camp, outlived its symbolic counterpart by several years.[16]

First published in 1933 when company 817 was at Stephenville, the bi-weekly *Blue Eagle News*, which billed itself as the oldest camp newspaper in Texas, continued in service at the McGregor site. Over the years, its columns recorded important information on construction projects, camp activities, personnel, special events, and the details of everyday life in the camp. Additionally, it provided a vehicle, albeit carefully reviewed, for the enrollees to express their viewpoints and to publish their own literary works. In the *Blue Eagle News*, and in the closed community it served, almost no story went unreported, which is why the preserved run of the camp newspaper is such an important historical record.

An article in April 1935 noted:

> The first [picnic] unit completed has a huge rock table with a top made up of three uniform pieces of unfinished white limestone with rock benches and unfinished rock fire place with wrought iron grills.
>
> The excavation for the Concession House, that is to be located at the south end of the park, is now complete.[17]

The same issue mentioned the camp truck, Big Bertha, a 3.5-ton 1918 model transferred from the Meridian camp, and noted the adoption of an honor system to reward enrollees who exhibited good citizenship and exemplary work ethics by granting them special passes or leaves.[18] Subsequent issues thanked the McGregor Fire Department for providing an emergency bell and the town's merchants for supplying baseball uniforms for the camp. There was also mention of the new superintendent, Captain W. K. Boggs, who temporarily took over the project during superintendent Byram's brief reassignment to Daingerfield. The article noted that Boggs held a commission in the 315th Engineers Reserve and that he had worked on projects at Caddo Lake, Graham, Goose Island, the Chisos Mountains (Big Bend), and Balmorhea before joining the company at Mother Neff.[19]

In July 1935, the paper included an article entitled "Enrollee Sits on a Snake," which described an encounter between a copperhead and a young man named "Scatter" Gray, remembered by others as one of the company's best mechanics:

> Glancing down he was more than moderately surprised to see the snake eject his head from under him. When the truck had quit vibrating and the dust had cleared, Scatter was none the worse except for numerous scratches made in the hasty exit and probable fang marks that failed to sufficiently penetrate his arm.[20]

There was the original poetry of enrollees such as Burt Gillis, who worked on the newspaper staff and also served as an assistant to the educational advisor:

Is It Love

The sun is brighter and the sky
Is bluer than before;
My heart is singing, for I've met
The girl that I adore.

The dew at morning, shining bright
Upon the grasses green,
Became the diamonds I'd bestow
Upon my lovely queen.

When day is closing and the clouds
Take on a brilliant hue,
The color's beauties seem to grow
At memories of you.[21]

Not all of the pieces were local; some, such as the "Psalm of the CCC," came from the national CCC newspaper, *Happy Days*:

The C.C.C. is my restoration; I shall not want,
But it maketh me arise early in the morning: it giveth
me baths with hard water.
It restoreth my appetite: it leadeth me in the paths
of work for my bankroll's sake.
Yea though I oft do K.P. duty from morn to night, I
will fear no evil, for the Infirmary is near me; the
oils and the pills they discomfort me.
Tables are prepared for me in the presence of my
buddies: my plate is heaped up; my stomach all but
runneth over.

> Surely goldbricking and tree nursing shall not fol-
> low me all the days of my life: but I shall probably
> remain in the CCC for ever.
>
> XEZ[22]

Such pieces about the CCC, which were obviously written in fun about life in the camp, were tolerated. It was seen as part of the esprit de corps that grew out of such close-quarter conditions. Articles that might present the CCC in a bad light, however, never made it past the ultimate editor, the base commander. Burt Gillis recalled one such incident:

> Marcus Dickey and I were two church boys, and we were interested in our fellows attending service when the chaplain would come. So, one time he came and he didn't have many out there. It was ridiculous with that many. So, boy, we sounded off in the Blue Eagle News. And that's when we shouldn't have done that, cause [Captain J. W. Oliver] called us both in. He said, "Now, I know you're going to tell it like it is. The thing of it is, we've got to think about the fact that we're dealing with the whole organization." And he said, "They'll be sending investigators down here, and all that kind of stuff, and we don't want that." And so he wanted that not to happen again. Of course, after that, Marcus and I were careful what we put in there.[23]

Viewed as a whole, the educational aspect of the CCC might be considered a failure at worst and a minimal achievement at best. While the various programs represented a noble experiment, established for the most part with the best of intentions and expectations, there were a number of factors that ultimately limited their effectiveness. From the beginning, the lack of support for a centralized and standardized program resulted in an amalgam of approaches, many initiated by inadequately or insufficiently trained company commanders and educational advisors. Where courses were offered on a regular basis, most were held in the evening hours, in the brief period of free time between supper and lights out. It is not surprising that young men, tired from a long day of demanding physical labor and not restricted by compulsory attendance concerns, often chose the camp recreation hall or the local towns over academic classes. Regardless, education in the CCC did make a difference in individual lives, allowing countless students to master basic elementary or high school skills, to pursue vocational interests, and even in some cases to seek a college degree. There were also those, influenced by their surroundings, who chose to join the military, or even the CCC, for employment. As the nation grew closer to war in the waning years of the CCC, others would have similar opportunities with regard to the military, although many would be motivated by more extrinsic factors such as the draft.

Entertainment, in its various manifestations, occupied most of the enrollees' free time. Frequently, there was little structure. The young men might gravitate to the recreation hall to listen to music, to smoke a cigarette, or just to visit. At Mother Neff, after 1936, many were drawn to the "rec hall" by the addition of a radio, which was still a strange and captivating technology to most of the boys. Those who had known about radio prior to their CCC service probably knew it in the form of the inexpensive crystal sets with their limited ranges and scratchy sounds. With the addition of the camp radio, however, the newspaper promised, "we can look forward to many long blissful P.M.s of dreamy music, comedy, drama, and all the things that come into our grasp through the medium. . . ."[24]

The CCC provided for unstructured leisure time, but understood that too much of a good thing could prove detrimental to the cause. Corps regulations prohibited the young men from having cars, although as was the case in most camps, many brought them to the area and then left them in the woods or on nearby farms for the occasional trips to town. Although Moody and McGregor were the closest towns of any size, the camp clearly developed within the McGregor sphere of influence. Robert Nettles told:

> We always went to McGregor. We never went to Moody. I guess McGregor was a little larger and had more to offer, which wasn't much. They had a dance hall where some of the guys went to load up on beer and get drunk and get in fights. I never did any of that. I didn't drink. I'd just go to a show, or go to a restaurant and eat some ice cream.[25]

Lore has it that the parents of Moody were perhaps more protective of their daughters and thus less receptive to the hordes of young men from the camp.

Drinking was one of those unstructured activities the CCC hoped to control, but seldom did. The young men of the CCC were no different from other teenagers and young adults of the time, and popular interests often included an occasional beer. Drinking was strictly prohibited in the camps, and public drunkenness was dealt with harshly by the camp administrators, leading some enrollees to protect their wayward buddies. Burt Gillis remembered such a time:

One of them came in there one night, drunk as he could be. Friend of mine. He laid down on the bunk. Cold, man it was cold outside, and we'd just turned the fire out. And you turned it out and left it out, it didn't make no difference what it was in there. So, he laid there on his bunk, and directly I heard him fall out on the floor. I thought to myself, if I leave him there overnight he'll be in the hospital. So, I got up, amid the protests of all the rest of them. I said, "Well, we can't leave him here." I said, "It's going to get colder and he's going to be freezing." So, I didn't have any help, but I pulled his shoes off. I didn't try to undress him, cause I figured in his condition he'd need all that clothing anyhow. I just turned the cover back over and he never moved the rest of the night, as far as I know. Boy, he liked to never got over me doing that, though. He knew I wouldn't be pulling a stunt like that. I said, "Well, I couldn't let you stay there." I said, "I was afraid you would really be sick." So, that gives you some idea of the closeness of the group.[26]

Despite the precautions of Moody parents, and others, there were many occasions when the CCC boys got together with local girls. Most encounters came in the form of organized activities such as dances and picnics, and romances, some lasting and some fleeting, would occasionally blossom. For the most part, these encounters were closely supervised or chaperoned, even by individuals other than the girl's immediate family. The story of Beulah Gamblin and Leon "Pancho" Anderson proves the point. The lovely Beulah, a Lion's Club Sweetheart, an accomplished piano player, and a whistler of some local renown, was invited to present her whistling act at the McGregor camp. In comparing herself to Ernest Tubb, she noted, "He waltzed all across Texas—I whistled all across Texas." She added:

> My favorite whistling tune was Glowworm ("Glow little glowworm, glimmer, glimmer. . .") and I went all out on it. Pancho was on the stage in one of the camp's little musical groups.
>
> He knew I wouldn't tell him my hometown so he was pretty slick. He asked me to get him the words to "Night and Day" and mail them to him. I did.
>
> To check on him, my parents had our pastor write his pastor. His pastor misunderstood and thought he was writing a job recommendation. He went all out in praising Pancho.[27]

Thanks to a winning "Glowworm" rendition and the intervention of two preachers, the couple were eventually united in marriage.

As previously noted, the local towns were, for the most part, supportive of the CCC's efforts at Mother Neff. Area residents frequently visited the park, even in its development stages, and participated in gatherings with the young men on occasion. Local churches often conducted services in the camp or provided transportation for camp members to join the regular worship services in town. Civic groups sometimes met in the park, as did local associations, such as the pecan growers' group. The camp newspaper recalled one such evening, when local Rotarians gathered with their wives to dance to the music of Dixie Dice's orchestra.[28]

The CCC camp was not without its musical and theatrical diversions. The *Blue Eagle News* regularly carried notices of special entertainment, much of which was provided by circuit performers, essentially vaudeville acts that traveled to the various CCC camps, as well as other venues, to put on reviews, stage shows, or plays. Those who visited the boys at McGregor included "Mr. and Mrs. Stevens," who performed "Ten Nights in a Bar Room" as part of the Don Compton Road Show, and the Imperial Vagabonds of Waco. There were also events that included talent shows, which gave camp members an opportunity to perform. One announcement included mention of the seven-piece orchestra from Waco's Hotel Roosevelt and added: "A specialty that drew heavy applause was a fast dance number by Smokey Joe Moss, colored enrollee of the company."[29]

Perhaps the biggest celebration that brought the town together with the young men of Company 817 was the Mother's Day celebration in 1935. Pat Neff organized the gala event to celebrate the CCC's work and to honor motherhood, his self-proclaimed personal inspiration for the park. Distinguished guests included the mothers of Governor James V. Allred and the singing Baylor quadruplets, the Keys sisters, billed as "the only college quadruplets in the world." Other notables in attendance were Governor Allred and State Parks Board members D. E. Colp, Judge Tom Beauchamp, and Gus Urbantke. Performers included the Baylor University Golden Wave Band and a black quartet from the CCC unit at Abilene State Park.[30]

A crowd estimated at 10,000 attended the day's events, which included a groundbreaking ceremony for the new clubhouse presided over by the governor, who in his remarks called mother love the "golden chord that binds the earth to God." Continuing on in praise of the particular mother's affection represented in the park's name, Allred added, "it is a monument not only to her, but to the motherhood of all Texas." Following his remarks, he took off his hat and coat and handed them to Mrs. A. H. Gregory of Gatesville, who at the age of 88 was the oldest woman present, and proceeded to turn the ceremonial spade of dirt. Overhead, airplanes from Randolph Field in San Antonio circled, taking pictures of the crowds throughout the day.[31]

Neff hoped to make the Mother's Day celebration an annual event at the park, which it was for several years. He also presided over Labor Day festivities, special Christmas programs, and other public gatherings. While he was no longer in political office, he remained a public figure, and the park events helped him to keep in touch with his many friends and former political supporters. He would come to rely on many of those connections in the future years through his continued association with the park and his dealings with the Texas State Parks Board.

Another form of camp entertainment that sometimes involved contact with local townspeople was sports, of both the structured and "sand lot" variety. The most popular games were the ones that took the least equipment: baseball, basketball, and boxing. Enrollees laid out a baseball diamond on land adjacent to the camp, and also set aside space for several basketball courts. Only occasionally did they have to realign them because of such natural hazards as rock outcroppings. By all accounts, the organized teams at Mother Neff were good, earning several pennants in district and regional competitions with other CCC camps and holding their own against local schools, such as Oglesby, Speegleville, and Eagle Springs. Company 817 also produced a number of boxing champions, some of whom successfully competed at the state level.[32] In addition to its status as a sport, boxing was sometimes used as a means of settling disputes between camp members. Officials preferred to end feuds in the boxing ring rather than on the job site, where the consequences could be much more serious.[33]

In addition to all of the structured and unstructured activities in the camp, there was also the casual, social interaction that resulted in lasting friendships. As Byron Culpepper remembered, "We became a family of brothers."[34] The enrollees had in common the economic condition of the depression years. Although some came from the same community or region of the state, there was some diversity. A 1935 roster of Company 817, for example, shows many boys from the Central Texas area (Marlin, Waco, Hamilton, Rosebud, Glen Rose, Hico, Lorena, and Hillsboro), but also some from South Texas (Edinburg and Kingsville), East Texas (Fostoria), and at least one other state (Arkansas). By and large, however, most came from an area that extended from the western edges of East Texas to the eastern limits of the Texas Hill Country. The majority of the young men were far enough from home that weekend visits were not economically feasible, and in some camps such distances led to desertion, a constant problem throughout the CCC.[35]

Each year of its existence, approximately 200 boys made the Mother Neff camp their home. Some served only temporarily, while others extended their tours for several years. In the course of their time with the CCC, most grew and matured, moving from boyhood into manhood. For the vast majority of the CCC boys, their camp experience marked an important benchmark in their lives and resulted in lifelong memories of good times, hard work, sacrifice, and lasting success. Perhaps no better example of personal growth and development at Mother Neff exists than the life history of one individual enrollee, Burt M. Gillis. His story is included here for a number of reasons, but most importantly because he provided an oral history which, when contrasted with his heartfelt writings in the *Blue Eagle News*, presents a poignant record of one young man's change over time.

Born in Kosse, Texas (Limestone County) in 1912, Gillis grew up on farms where his sharecropping parents picked cotton on the "halves." Those families who had their own equipment and animals might pick on rented land and return a fourth (fourths) to the landowner in return for their home. Those who had less, and the least, and thus had to rely on the added support of the landowner, had to turn over half the crop. In the economic hierarchy of the sharecropping system, where often differences were subtle but clearly understood, the "halvers" were at the bottom. Gillis recalled those tough times:

> I remember one thing that stands out, and that was that one afternoon some friends of ours came up out in front of the house and I was in the back, doing some kind of chore. I had on my old work clothes, and they were so ragged that I wouldn't go around to the front. I'll remember that if I live to be a hundred. I didn't want them to see me.[36]

When Burt was sixteen, his father died, leaving a widow and four children. As the oldest son, Burt had to quit school and look for additional work to provide money for the family. He remembered the parting admonishment from his principal: "Gillis, if you'd been able to get an education, you might have amounted to something, but I don't know about it now." Resolute, the young man thought, "I'll show you."[37]

At the age of eighteen, Gillis left home to work on a road gang. It was at this time in his life that he began to think about a lifetime career, possibly as a preacher. Some people had told him he "looked like one," but he had not yet had that spiritual "calling." There were signs, however, and every rural boy knew about the importance of making important decisions, such as planting and harvesting, by the signs.

> One night I was out under the stars. I just said, "lord, if I'm to preach, let me see a star shoot across. And just as I thought it, it did. But, the old devil came along and said, "Oh, stars shoot across all the time, don't you know that?"[38]

Eventually, Gillis learned about the CCC, possibly through his landlord, and joined up at a water conservation project near Coolidge, in northern Limestone County. From there, he was transferred to the Mother Neff park, arriving near the end of 1935. He was then 23 years old, without a formal education, and without a clear career goal. He must have had talent, though, since he quickly became associate editor of the *Blue Eagle News*. Shortly after his arrival and new assignment, he wrote a poem called "Our Many Laws":

> There's a law on roads
> And a law on speeds;
> There's a law on bills
> And a law on deeds.
>
> There's a law on drink
> We never did keep;
> There's a law on dogs
> And a law on sheep.

There are laws and laws
For each little thing,
For the fish in streams
And the birds on wing.

But we'll admit
That the greatest law
Is the Law on laws,
To obey the law.[39]

Much of Gillis's writings reflect the inner searching he was experiencing at the time. They speak of spiritual matters, of nature, of friendships, and of his respect for the opportunities he had been given. In the summer of 1936, he wrote the following:

Memories of CCC Days

I'll miss it when I'm gone,
That camp beside the way
That place where day by day
New friends were won.

I'll miss the comradeship,
Of those it sheltered there,
For in a certain sense,
We were as one.

In after days there'll be,
A memory that's strong,
Of how we worked and played,
Within that place.

And though we go our ways,
Between us there are ties,
That time and circumstance
May ne'er erase.

So let us hope that when
This life has come and gone
That we shall meet with Christ
In realms above.

Within a joyful home,
Where hate has ceased to be,
We shall forever dwell,
In perfect love.[40]

The following month, Gillis and enrollee Evan Miller represented Company 817 at the Texas Centennial in Dallas. There, as part of a public display on the CCC in the state, they exhibited examples of the camp coppersmithing classes, as well as copies of the *Blue Eagle News*.[41]

Gillis's writings in the camp newspaper the following year show a continued longing for answers. But, as the closing words of the poem, "After Sundown," reveal, there was also a peace borne of faith:

I hear the tender, loving call;
Of one who watches over all;
In humble huts or mansions tall;
Just after the sun goes down.

He tells me life is not in vain;
That all will soon be right again;
He gives my heart a glad refrain,
Just after the sun goes down.[42]

A couple of months later, in April 1937, Gillis and other camp members participated in a special open house celebration at the camp. To honor the event, which over 3,000 people attended, several enrollees, including Gillis, represented Company 817 "on the air." Broadcast on station WACO, the radio program featured a speech by Captain Oliver and several musical numbers, including an original by Gillis entitled "I Cling to His Hand."[43]

As the summer of 1937 ended, there were rumors that the CCC would soon be shut down. Congress called for severe cutbacks, and over half of Company 817 prepared to be discharged. Among those facing life back in the real world was Burt Gillis, who penned a poignant final piece:

> Farewell to the CCC,
> Where we lived and worked and played,
> Where many a thing was learned,
> And many a friend was made.
>
> Farewell to the CCC,
> Where the nation's youth was met,
> Where many a tie was forged,
> That many can ne'r forget.
>
> Farewell to the CCC.
> Where the nation's boys made men,
> Where many a one formed strength,
> Renewing their hope within.
>
> Farewell to the CCC.
> We will part, but meet again,
> Wherever our paths may cross,
> To share our joy and pain.[44]

During his time at Mother Neff, young Burt Gillis must have looked at the stars countless times, but never asked the right question. Following his service with the CCC, he began working for a bakery in Waco. One evening, after attending a revival, he found the courage he needed. While sleeping outside, he recalled:

> I looked up at the stars; starry, clear night. Thought back to when I was eighteen years old. I was twenty-five then. Thought about when I saw a star shoot across as a sign I ought to be in the ministry. And just as I thought it, it did."[45]

Buoyed once again by the signs, he soon enrolled as a "special student" at Baylor with much support and encouragement, and personal blessing, from Pat Neff. Perhaps drawing on his CCC experience, he persisted, graduated, and then enrolled in seminary courses by correspondence. Eventually, the *Reverend* Burt Gillis fulfilled his "call" and became a well-respected Methodist preacher, a position he held actively for over thirty years. And, his companion throughout that time, and more, was his wife, Adele, the young lady he met as an enrollee and whose love he addressed in a camp newspaper poem so many years before.

The story of the Rev. Burt Gillis is unique, as was the personal story of each individual who served with Company 817 at the Mother Neff camp, but it is also representative of the changes countless young men experienced during their years with the CCC. Collectively, the stories speak of an organization that provided them with timely opportunities, that turned boys into men, that taught them skills, and that prepared them for the future. The CCC had its problems, as well as its detractors, but it also had an abundance of personal successes. Perhaps no

better commendation is due the organization than the reflective thoughts of Burt Gillis about the integrity of the unit: "I
don't know of any enrollee who turned out bad after he left that
camp. Some of them were more successful than others, but none
of them became criminals or got in trouble with the law."[46] Such
praise helps form the foundation of continued efforts even to
this day to resurrect, or recreate in some other manifestation,
the positive impact of the organization. As historian Arthur M.
Schlesinger, Jr., observed, the CCC "left its monuments in the
preservation and purification of the land, the water, the forests,
and the young men of America"[47]—important words to remember for those who now, generations later, enjoy the structures,
the roads, and the pathways of parks such as Mother Neff.

5

Politics and a Park

Throughout its brief history, the CCC had to contend with a number of individuals, on all levels of operation, who wanted more from the organization than it could deliver, legally, ethically, or administratively. There were those who called for such changes as innovative educational programs, full integration of the service, military instruction, and permanent status. As a result, the CCC attracted more than its fair share of activists, from religious leaders and educators to social workers and nutritionists. There was one group, however, that superseded all the others in intensity and direct involvement. They were the politicians.

From its inception, the CCC was political. In theory and intent, at least, it was designed to be separate from political maneuverings. Its successes, however, eventually opened it to outside influences, and politicians from city councils to congressmen were quick to realize the exploitative potential. Few could resist the siren song of the corps in the era of economic uncertainty. Its effectiveness in bringing relief to young men and their families, as well as to scarred and depleted lands, made CCC camps coveted political plums. And in the earliest part of Roosevelt's new federalism, such plums were a rare delicacy to be savored—and preserved.

As a direct result of political pressure, CCC projects were often truncated in favor of work in more politically sensitive areas of the nation. Companies were moved in and out of projects, disbanded and reorganized, and split into side camps in order to spread the effectiveness and maximize the presence of the program. Always aware of their reliance on congressional support, despite the enthusiastic endorsement of the president, the cooperating agencies (NPS, USDA, etc.) were frequently guilty of trying to appease too many with too few men and too little funding. While the CCC enjoyed unprecedented bipartisan support in its early years, it never achieved permanent status, nor did it grow beyond certain imposed limitations that, at times, included the budget, size considerations, and program restrictions. It was, in effect, a social experiment, and the threat of termination was a constant and pervasive influencing factor in both location and program considerations.

So intense was the competition for CCC projects that when they eventually ran their course, for whatever reason, most local officials turned to political pressure to retain them. Rumors of transfer abounded in the CCC, and when news of a proposed relocation leaked out to the local citizenry, it often triggered a flurry of correspondence, phone calls, petitions, newspaper editorials, and meetings, both private and public. Sometimes the rumors were unfounded. Sometimes, however, they were merely political trial balloons, designed to either stir up or test local support. More often the rumors were based in truth, although the details of timing and subsequent projects might remain conjectural for months. Regardless, it often fell to the politicians to attempt to remedy the situation.

A typically dramatic response to rumors of a camp closure was for local or state officials to call upon their elected representatives in Washington to intervene personally with the CCC and with administrators of cooperating agencies, or with anyone else who might be able to effect change. In some cases, local officials even made well-publicized trips to the nation's capital in order to "personally" tend to the matter. No politician was immune to this type of constituent support, and throughout the course of the CCC there must have been a steady stream of political contingents making their way to the national offices. And the CCC offices were not the only destination for these contingents; depending on the nature of the project, they might try to meet with departmental leaders, or even with the president. The fact that some managed to achieve their objectives and extend the work of local camps only influenced others to try. Future president Lyndon Johnson, a congressman from Texas in the late 1930s, was one of those who succeeded. No stranger to power politics even then, Johnson was able to persuade NPS officials to expand the role of Company 854, which was at the time completing an assignment at Longhorn Cavern in Burnet County in the Texas Hill Country. In a letter to Burnet mayor Thomas C. Ferguson that was reprinted in the local newspaper, Johnson noted:

> After appeal to Secretary [Harold] Ickes [Interior Department] and [Robert] Fechner [CCC director], retention of Longhorn Cavern State Park Camp has been approved. Upon my return to Texas, Park Board, CRA [Colorado River Authority], and representatives of the National Park Service will meet

and attempt to acquire acreage in vicinity of Inks
Lake for development.[1]

The associated newspaper article recorded, "This is the second
time that he [Johnson] has prevailed upon the powers that be to
keep the CC Camp in this county after orders for its removal
had been made."[2] The result of the congressman's personal efforts was the development of Inks Lake State Park, now one of
the most popular recreational areas within the state park system.

Where Johnson succeeded many others failed, and CCC companies were moved and reorganized continually as part of the national program. Consequently, projects were often abandoned before completion, and the argument of "unfinished business" became a rallying point for those attempting to retain the CCC camps.
In some instances, that too paid off. In 1934, the CCC withdrew
Company 1823V, a company comprised of unemployed white
military veterans, from work on the Lake Abilene park project near
Buffalo Gap in Taylor County and transferred them to a similar
project at Sweetwater in Nolan County. Then, in April 1935, corps
officials reorganized the company into a unit for black veterans, the
first of its kind in Texas. The change in unit makeup did not meet
with the favor of Sweetwater city leaders, and they formally noti-
fied the agency of their opposition to the black enrollees in their
vicinity. Since the CCC required the support of local governments
in order to retain a camp, they were left with a unit that had no
project and thus no home.

The citizenry of Abilene, eager for completion of their nearby
state park, responded quickly. As the newspaper reported:

Sweetwater protested on two grounds: (1) Nolan
County's negro population is small, and (2) In the

> Lake Sweetwater park area forty or fifty cabins have
> been built, these being occupied over weekends by
> families of the owners. The Lake Abilene area on
> the other hand is secluded, the nearest towns, Buf-
> falo Gap and Tuscola, being five or six miles away.[3]

Abilene mayor C. L. Johnson activated the city's task force on the CCC, which reportedly "canvassed" local residents on their opinions about having a black veterans group finish the work at Lake Abilene. As the newspaper article noted, "All questioned said 'no objection.' " Although it is doubtful the response was either comprehensive or unanimous, as the article implied, local officials pressed on, formally notifying their congressman, Thomas L. Blanton, and others of their interest:

> We respectfully request that you inform Director
> Fechner that Abilene will be delighted to have the
> negro CCC camp now located at Lake Sweetwater
> transferred to Lake Abilene park to complete the
> work there. The camp will receive a welcome. We
> prefer this camp right now rather than taking a
> chance on getting another later. Sentiment here suf-
> ficiently determined to warrant this request to you.[4]

Blanton and Fechner both responded favorably in short order, and the company, by then known as 1823CV ("colored veterans"), albeit reorganized, returned to its previous assignment at Lake Abilene.

At Mother Neff State Park, the response to rumors of relocation was no less political or intense than those evidenced at Abilene, Burnet, and countless other projects throughout the CCC system. It was perhaps more personal, however, given the historical association and direct involvement of Pat Neff, then chairman of the State Parks Board. Although the camp had far outlived its initial projected work schedule of eighteen to twenty-four months, Neff was not willing to let it go without a fight. Using the standard response of unfinished business, he contacted a number of leaders, including the influential Washington representatives from the Heart of Texas area, Representative W. R. Poage and Senator Tom Connally. He also enlisted the assistance of others in similar efforts, and his influence can be seen in their correspondence. A letter from O. T. McGinley, vice president of the McGregor Chamber of Commerce, to Representative Poage in 1938 includes attachments composed on a different typewriter. Although no name is listed on the attachments, they could well have been written by Neff, or with his assistance.

> It seems that it would have, perhaps, been better if CCC Camp 817 had never been stationed at Mother Neff State Park if the park is to be abandoned in its present unfinished state. As a completed park, Mother Neff State Park will be one of the most beautiful and most visited parks in our state, but if left unfinished it will soon become one of those forgotten parks, and all the time, pain-taking [sic] care, and money will have been spend [sic] in vain.[5]

Among the projects the Mother Neff camp supporters elaborated on as unfinished business were the removal of underbrush for fire safety considerations, replacement of playground equipment, completion of the main entryway, construction of parking areas, treatment of diseased trees, and, prophetically, development of flood control systems. They even pleaded their case for architectural changes to the new park structures, most notably the pavilion:

> With the idea of good landscaping in mind, some technician employed by the National Park Service insisted on locating the Recreation Pavilion within thirty feet of the banks of the Leon River. Though it is true this makes a very beautiful site, it is proved to be a dangerous location. Due to the fact that when the Leon River rises and goes down, the banks . . . are eaten way about four feet each year. At this rate it will only be a short time until the building is undermined and will be a total loss. It is believed that it will take the entire company three months to correct this condition in a safe, efficient manner.[6]

Another park project Neff considered unfinished was one that he had successfully lobbied for earlier: a new route to the park that eventually became known as the Old River Road. Although it was not officially a CCC project, the road was essential to park development in his view. In a 1937 letter to Judge Robert Lee Bobbitt, chairman of the State Highway Commission, he wrote:

> You may recall that I appeared before the Commission at its last meeting in Austin, on behalf of a Community-Marketing road running South from Oglesby in Coryell County, Northeast of the Leon River as far South as Mother Neff Park and circling back in a loop by the ancient village of Eagle Springs.
>
> I am enclosing herein a resolution signed by members of the Chamber of Commerce of Oglesby, and stating the need of such a road from the stand-

point of a marketing road, a school bus line and a community enterprise. I do not know of any place more sadly in need of an outlet for Church, School and Marketing purposes than the section covered by this proposed route. . . . The road would be a great help to the students of the Eagle Springs Community where I went to school as a bare-foot boy.[7]

Neff believed the work still to be completed at Mother Neff, including the road, would take an additional two years. While this must have seemed improbable even to him, given what he knew of the National Park Service and its priorities, he nonetheless persisted with deliberate haste and political pressure. He was buoyed in that regard by a letter from William J. Lawson, executive secretary of the State Parks Board—in effect, Neff's employee on the board—who had advocated continued camp presence at both Mother Neff and Garner state parks. Calling Neff's attention to pending appropriations debates in Congress, Lawson wrote in a letter:

From the conversations we had with Mr. [Conrad] Wirth [of the National Park Service], I am convinced that the retention or removal of any CCC Camp is purely a political matter and not based upon any system of merit or stage of completion of any park. I believe, personally, that if I had as many political contacts in Washington as you have, with such men as Vice President [John Nance] Garner, Senators [Tom] Connally and [Morris] Sheppard and a multitude of Congressmen, that I would play the same game that the National Park Service Officials are playing and enlist the aid of some of these friends.[8]

Neff needed little encouragement and obviously no instruction on matters political, but he apparently took Lawson's advice to heart. Like many other committed citizens and officials across the nation facing the closure of nearby CCC camps, Neff made a trip to Washington to plead his case in person. He traveled to the capital in May 1938, and although he was successful in arranging a number of key meetings, he apparently came quickly to the conclusion that Mother Neff State Park would not be completed, at least in the foreseeable future, by the young men of the CCC. The closing of the camp was a foregone conclusion by that summer.[9]

Following his Washington trip, Neff began to change his tactics, perhaps because the NPS had promised to direct a side camp from the Cleburne project, under the direction of Company 3804, to complete several projects. With that assurance, he then began working to retain the camp facilities in hopes that the CCC might eventually return or that another agency might be moved in to work on the park. Both the National Youth Administration and the U. S. Army had options on the barracks, which were actually owned by the army, and both initially planned to remove them from the park. The army exercised their ownership in July, but noted they would take no action to dismantle or remove the structures until the termination of the side camp. National Park Service inspector W. F. Ayres wrote in September:

> Since visiting the park, I have discussed this matter with Superintendent Byram of the Cleburne State Park and Lieutenant Mannley, Adjutant of the North Texas District CCC with a view to extending the life of this side camp until January 1, 1939. This will be agreeable to the Army Authorities and Su-

perintendent Byram can spare the men now engaged.
I would like authority from this Service to extend
this camp for the next three months to complete
this last job [trails, walkways, parking lot, roads, and
guard rails]. All of the material is on hand with the
exception of some stone. . . .[10]

Following correspondence with the NYA state director, J.
C. Kellam, Neff believed that agency would eventually relinquish its claim to the barracks. A subsequent letter from William J. Lawson, in which he again offered the governor his personal political advice, revealed otherwise:

It seems that the National Youth Administration has double crossed you. It was my understanding that they had given you their promise that they
would not claim the CCC buildings at the Mother
Neff Park.

I am today in receipt of the attached memoran-
dum from the Regional Office which shows that the
N.Y.A. has claimed all of the buildings which had
been promised to the Texas State Parks Board. This
means that nothing whatever will be left in this camp
in the way of CCC buildings. . . . Time is of the
essence in this matter and I believe if I were you I
would phone the N.Y.A. office by long distance.[11]

And, once again, Neff followed the advice, contacting both
the army and the NYA, as he revealed in a letter only a few days
later:

Now, in regard to the buildings at Mother Neff Park,
desire to say that the Army positively refuses to re-

linquish these buildings and they have demolished
most of them. The N.Y.A. organization, however,
that did not relinquish its right after the organization found that the Army was going to take them
advised the Army authorities that the N.Y.A. organization was desirous of retaining a portion of some
of the buildings. In a quiet way the N.Y.A. organization told me that if they could get possession of
these buildings that they might be able to work out
something of mutual interest with us. The attitude
of the N.Y.A. organization is cooperative, but the
Army spoke as an Army.[12]

The "mutual interest" deal that Neff worked out with the
NYA apparently called for the buildings to be retained for an
NYA camp at Mother Neff, and that the camp would oversee
the completion of CCC projects in the park. The National Youth
Administration had an organizational structure and mission not
unfamiliar to Neff. Established by executive order as part of
Roosevelt's New Deal in 1935, two years after the CCC, it was
also designed to promote work projects and jobs for young
people. The NYA was, however, more open in its approach,
promoting access by more diverse groups, including minorities
and women, and emphasizing education, especially an appreciation for democratic principles. The organization worked
through local school programs at both the high school and college levels to involve active students as well as dropouts. Unlike
the CCC that housed enrollees exclusively in isolated, military-
type camps away from their homes, the NYA also utilized "resident training centers," where students either stayed for brief
periods of time, perhaps a summer, or worked after hours during the school year. While the NYA worked on such projects as

roads, bridges, and public buildings, including schools and libraries, the resident centers became, in effect, industrial trade schools, and graduates were often hired by local industries, especially as war preparedness increased in the early 1940s.[13]

The NYA used the former CCC facilities at Mother Neff State Park as a training center for a group of young girls from the Temple area. While their time commitment and workforce levels (about 20) were limited, the NYA girls cleared campsites, constructed associated facilities, and built a series of cottages which were to be rented to park visitors. In a 1940 letter, Neff elaborated:

> I made a trade with the NYA people while I was a member of the Board that if they would move in there and use the old timber that had been left, I would buy all the new timber necessary and all the nails, roofing, and other things they might need in building a number of cottages in the park. With that understanding, the NYA organization has been in the Park for more than a year using up this old lumber, old doors, and old window frames wherever possible in building some new cottages, a recreation hall, a bathhouse, and some other buildings incidental to these. In an effort to carry out my part of the contract with the NYA I have spent over $600 of my money on these new cottages. For the new recreation hall that they are building up where the old camp was originally located I furnished the major part of what is going into it.[14]

Neff was not one to ask for reimbursement for his personal expenses, but he was also not above letting others know of his contributions. In later dealings with the State Parks Board, his itemization of donations became more frequent and more detailed. Continuing his letter, he provided additional information about the work of the NYA girls:

> This NYA organization is building at this time two cottages down at the pavilion section of the Park and I have asked them to build three others in that section of the Park using the old lumber where they could and I am still financing them for other necessary materials.
>
> We have rented these cottages recently built and some two buildings belonging originally to the camp there to people who are working on a new road that leads into the Park down through the Leon river bottom on the North coming in from Oglesby [the Old River Road]. . . . These buildings were not put up by the Parks Board or by the State and I thought it would not be improper for us to rent them to these workers to help pay in some small way for the expenses incurred in the erecting of buildings there on the old camp site. It is true these buildings could be torn down and probably old lumber used somewhere else, but the buildings consist of the old blacksmith shop, the office building, and a couple of shacks which seem to me would be of far more value to be left in the Park where they are, notwithstanding that they belong to the Parks Board, than to be torn down and used elsewhere.[15]

Neff's detailed letter provides more insights into post-CCC park operations than just his elaborations on the agreement with the NYA. It also shows his continued personal involvement, his determination to make major operational decisions, and his unwillingness to turn over operations to parks board personnel. In fact, Neff had himself named park superintendent upon leaving the State Parks Board in 1939, and he ran the site almost as a personal business. He opened a store in the concession building, hired sisters Marie and Tullie Jones to manage the operation, and loaned them money to purchase inventory and supplies. In his letter of employment to the women, he wrote:

> As a rental, you are to pay $5 per month for the year designated. It is understood that you may pay this rental at intervals as will suit your convenience. . . . You are to pay the electric light bills for the store and for the pavilion, it being understood also that the money put into the meters for the operation of the lights at the pavilion is to belong to you. . . . You are to keep the tables and chairs used in connection with the store clean and properly placed at all times and to have general supervision of the store and those who use it as a gathering place. . . . You will recall that the State Parks Board has not at any time invested anything in these groceries and it has no interest in them. They were purchased by me in order that the store might be operated on a cash basis relying on the understanding that I would be reimbursed from time to time for this advancement made.[16]

Neff also hired Claude Jones, brother of the Jones sisters, as park caretaker, paying his salary of twenty dollars a month out of the twenty-five appropriated by the Parks Board for monthly salary needs, plus other considerations. In correspondence with

Jones, Neff spelled out other details of the financial agreement. In addition to his salary, the caretaker would be provided lodging in the park and would receive half the park income, other than that brought in by the store. Such income included cabin rentals, table reservations, and "the sale of anything pertaining to the Park for which a charge may be made." The other fifty percent of the funds went toward park maintenance. For the sum of $250, Neff also allowed Jones to become part owner in a pickup which the caretaker used for park business.[17]

In addition to his maintenance responsibilities, Jones was also expected to work for his employer on other personal projects as needed and to supervise loosely the work of his sisters. It is not clear if they knew about the latter, however. Neff wrote to his caretaker in September 1939:

> While it is not a part of our contract, you were a witness to the trade made with your two sisters in reference to the operation of the store in the Park. While the contract was made with the girls, we recognize that you are largely responsible for the operation of the store and the girls will work in a large measure under your direction. The contract, however, is with the girls and I am not counting on you devoting any time to the store more than to counsel with the girls and to assist them in getting commodities to the store.[18]

Neff apparently preferred to purchase equipment and to handle most other financial matters on his own rather than having to deal with the Parks Board. He funded such items as landscaping materials, tools, construction equipment, the use of "hired hands" from his nearby farm, and, of course, his share of the park truck. He would, from time to time, remind the board of his generosity, especially when he was at odds with them about matters related to the park. And that was frequent and consistent.[19]

In a particularly lengthy and detailed letter to the State Parks Board in August 1939, Neff provided specifics about his numerous contributions. His enumerations included fencing, household furnishings, a stove and icebox, electricity, groceries for the store, and lumber for the NYA work, in all totaling $1406.17. But, he reminded the board, "Nothing that I did, however, has placed any financial obligations upon the Board." In typical Neff fashion, he added an understated qualifier: "Although I feel that it is my park, I am conscious of the fact that it belongs to the State and that I have no more authority in it than any other citizen."[20]

In such correspondence to the board, Neff often wrote from a defensive frame of reference. Typical is his response to criticism about his park maintenance program, which was minimal at best. Attempting to divert attention from his shortcomings, he instead attacked the attitude of the inspector who filed the damning report. In a vitriolic letter, he chided the park official for his use of "sulphurous English," and for cursing "in the old fashioned way about everything that is going on at the Park." He added, "From the description given to me this party must at some time have worked for the Federal Government."[21]

The February 1940 letter that mentioned the impious park official was one of Neff's most heated and condescending. In it, he brought to bear all his emotions about the park and about the obvious neglect he perceived on the part of the Texas State Parks Board. Their disinterest or inability to provide the changes the former governor thought were necessary to enhance the park's

potential as a major tourist attraction were, to him, unforgiv-
able. So too, perhaps, was what he saw as their lack of allegiance
to the man who had provided their means of employment
through creation of the board decades earlier. And to add insult
to injury, their criticism of his operations made him furious. He
saw their concerns as nit-picking. Apparently asked to account
for money he collected in rentals, including the boarding of
mules for the road contractor, Neff replied, "Now, if we happen
to make $100 or $200 during the year from these little rentals
and things of that kind, I do not think, in view of the [personal]
expenditure, that anyone ought to complain about having in
and around the park a few things that will bring in a small
amount of money."[22] Neff viewed his relationship with the board
as something of a ledger sheet, and as long as the balance was in
his favor, he felt justified in his actions.

A good example of Neff's maverick attitude was his introduction of farmyard livestock into the park, including the camping area:

> My plan is to fill the park with chickens, geese, tur-
> keys, pigions [sic], peafowls, and any other similar
> fowls, and that these added to the goats and sheep
> will make the park more interesting. . . . I cannot
> think of anything more interesting than 1000 white
> chickens and 100 Angora goats inhabiting the woods
> and browsing on the prairie of the Park.[23]

Neff eventually acquiesced somewhat on the animal issue
after park visitors complained of frequent and disturbing encounters, primarily with the goats and geese. His solution was
to construct animal pens on the upper end of the park, near
where the CCC camp had been located, and to provide a mea-

sure of containment behind a fence that crossed at the southern wooded edge of the large open prairie. Neff also gave in on other issues, most notably on his plan to construct a Baptist church within the park. Although he lost some battles, he won many others, and thus kept the scales tipped in his favor.

Neff's control of his old family park went virtually unchecked through the war years of the 1940s. His attention to park operations included numerous personal promotions. Neff was perhaps aware, even in the early days of the park, that his beloved family grounds would not become the major tourist attraction he had envisioned, especially without some promotional pressure. Although he would never have admitted it, he must have seen that its relatively small size, its propensity for flooding, its location off major travel routes, and its distance from developing urban centers would limit its popularity. Maybe the vision he had for parks in the 1920s as community gathering places and points of inspiration was already becoming outdated by the latter part of the 1930s at the advent of an urbanized, mobile society. Certainly he realized that if his park was to compete successfully with others, his perseverance and enthusiasm, coupled with his charisma and his standing as a prominent politician, educator, and religious lay leader, were essential to attracting visitors. Even though he may have had doubts at times, he never let go of his vision. He continued to feel that if he could share the park with enough people, they would be charmed by the peaceful setting of the Leon valley and by the CCC's rustic architectural landscape. And once they had experienced the park, they would return and bring others with them.

The love Neff had for his park and for its neighbors guided his early promotions, which seemed to represent a return to the community gatherings, family reunions, revivals, and chautauquas of his memories. In March 1939, he wrote of plans to have a local school reunion at the park. He wrote to a former classmate, asking his assistance in contacting "'old timers' who went to school at Eagle Springs, who carried corn to be ground at Whitson's Mill, and who, in our day and generation, circulated in and around the neighborhood of Mother Neff Park and Eagle Springs." He poignantly added, "Now, what I want you to do is to help me round up those individuals with whom we played mumblepeg and other similar games. . . ."[24] He followed that with another special Mother's Day celebration in May in which he formally presented the newly completed park to the State Parks Board. In June, he sought assistance from the McGregor Chamber of Commerce and the Rotary club for another community function:

> I am very eager for the Park to be used, especially by the people in the towns and the counties around. . . . I thought I would ask several of the towns that it serves to sponsor, now and then, some character of a gathering in the Park. The Park is identified with McGregor more than any other town. Therefore, I am asking McGregor if it will sponsor a Fourth of July picnic this coming Fourth of July. I want it to be a McGregor picnic, held at Mother Neff State Park, rather than just a picnic at Mother Neff Park. In other words, I want it to be McGregor's picnic held in the Park. I will not ask you to do anything like this again for at least five years.[25]

By the 1940s, the nation's collective interest had turned to war preparedness, and even rural areas like the countryside around Mother Neff State Park were affected by the change.

Some parks virtually shut down during the war years, but others, like Mother Neff State Park, literally "boomed" because of their proximity to wartime development. Not far from Mother Neff, the U. S. Army began developing massive Fort Hood, and even closer was the Bluebonnet Ordnance Plant at McGregor. Eventually, the government would establish other military installations in nearby towns. Support industries and businesses also developed, and soon there was a shortage of housing in Coryell County. Neff did his part to help by opening the park cottages, at least on a temporary basis, to workers. He even responded graciously, and perhaps with a bit of facetiousness, to a suggestion from a local civil defense officer that the park be used as a "haven of refuge" for those who might find themselves homeless as a result of "enemy air raids, serious fire or other calamity."[26] Neff answered diplomatically, "I desire to say that when life, for any reason, becomes hazardous in the town of McGregor, Mother Neff State Park will gladly open her gates to all McGregorites."[27] Neff's support of the war effort apparently had its limits, however. When asked by the State Parks Board to contribute all available park materials of copper, brass, and bronze for a metal drive, he responded, "we have looked over Mother Neff State Park and do not find any material of this nature."[28] Thus were possibly saved from the scrap heap many of the ornate metal furnishings and commemorative tablets that were significant elements of the CCC contributions.

During the war years, Neff became less of a regular fixture at the park. He began to tend to other pressing matters, leaving the questions of park operations to the staff of the Texas State Parks Board. His correspondence about the park dropped dramatically during the war, but what has remained shows he had additional, and significant, plans for the site. In a 1945 letter to Norfleet G. Bone of the Texas State Parks Board, Neff wrote:

> As I stated to you in our previous conversation at the Park some days ago, it would be my real pleasure to meet you there at almost any time that would suit you. I would like to go over not only the original park, but I would also be delighted to go over with you the 1400 acres of land that is to be added to the Park even though the Park will not come into actual possession of it for some years.[29]

The additional land donation, evidently to be a gift from the governor's estate upon his death, never materialized, and his beloved little park remained much as he knew it during his lifetime.

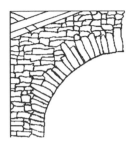

6

Back to Nature

The Second World War brought a tidal wave of recreation visitors to Mother Neff State Park. When the State Parks Board first documented attendance at its New Deal developments, Mother Neff recorded 16,504 visitors for the season (May through September 1937). Excluding that Depression summer's astounding 252,000 patrons of MacKenzie State Park in Lubbock (where a huge and inviting swimming pool attracted bathers from far and wide), the Neff park figures compared favorably with others, such as Tyler State Park at 12,900 and Brownwood State Park's 10,250. In May 1945, as the parks opened for their last wartime season, gatekeepers at Tyler counted 9,600, while Brownwood served 8,300, and Mother Neff—half the size of Tyler and one-quarter the acreage at Lake Brownwood—welcomed 6,880 visitors that month alone.[1]

All these outlandish figures revealed proximity of heavily populated military bases near the parks, as Tyler served Camp Fannin and Brownwood hosted Camp Bowie. Mother Neff State

Park drew a constant stream of visitors from two large installations, Camp Hood sprawling a few miles to the southwest and small but booming Bluebonnet Ordnance Plant a short distance north on the road to McGregor.

Pat Neff's dream for his Leon River park to be recognized as a mainstream destination near a major circulation corridor for Texas had seemingly come true. Upon its completion in 1938 Mother Neff State Park featured more day-use structures than most similar parks in the bustling system. The massive CCC effort to raise its river-bottom campground above normal flood levels supposedly made this park available throughout the summer season in most any weather. And now its fine collection of National Park Service-designed facilities—two pavilions, the refectory, cottages and picnic clusters, large-capacity water system, and a grand caretaker's lodge—served admirably under the weight of heavy visitation brought by a wartime boom.

Under these taxing conditions, in August 1945 parks board landscape architect Norfleet Bone found the park in remarkably good repair. In his inspection report, with copy provided to President Neff at Baylor, Bone noted repairs needed to plumbing, roofs, and picnic areas. He "found Governor Neff[,] and the custodians looking after the park[,] most enthusiastic and interested in the proper operation and maintenance of the area," among impressions of a well arranged park. Claude Jones, doubling as park manager and foreman of Pat Neff's adjacent 2,200-acre farm, continued this arrangement crafted by Neff years before and encompassing several other members of the Jones family. To increase efficiency in the Joneses' park enterprise, Bone recommended acquisition of a "motor vehicle" and "power mowing equipment," plus a "Row boat for use of custodian during floods," the latter an unfortunate admission that Mother Neff park suffered periodic rises of the Leon River.

Then, that very month, the war ended. Mother Neff's home-front patronage departed early for the summer season and the defense-training and industrial census of the region plummeted. Nearby McGregor's population fell from 6,000 to 2,000 by year's end, and Killeen—at the gateway to Camp Hood—dropped from 7,000 back to its pre-war habitation of 1,200. Thus the visitor figures for Mother Neff State Park at its season opening in May 1946 returned to a few hundred patrons per month.[2]

Overall the State Parks Board weathered this dramatic shift quite well, benefiting from healthy wartime state-revenue surpluses and from an increasingly supportive legislature. For its 1946 budget, the Texas system of thirty-seven parks received a substantial increase to more than $120,000, and most of its employees earned a fifteen percent raise. The annual salary for Mother Neff's custodian—Claude Jones and family—rose to $900, plus free accommodations in the keeper's residence; and the park showed a $400 annual maintenance budget. In reality, the latter funds would be pooled with similar individual park appropriations, and no major improvements would be scheduled in the near future at Mother Neff, other than repairs noted during Norfleet Bone's visit. But with its combined budgets and substantial concession profits, the parks board placed priority on post-war construction at a number of state parks from Cleburne to Possum Kingdom, plus the new Bentsen-Rio Grande Valley State Park.

In tragic contrast, austere wartime budget cuts for the National Park Service, one-time benevolent partner to Texas in design and construction of New Deal parks including Mother

Neff, endured even beyond war's end. During the peak of their own facility developments between 1933 and 1940, national parks visitation had leaped from two million to sixteen million. But from an astonishing high of twenty-one million patrons the next year, including the last summer before Pearl Harbor, dramatic drops in bureau budgets and severe restrictions on leisure travel starting in 1942 allowed only six million Americans to visit national parks that first war year. Then, with the federal government's commitment to "reconversion" of the economy, "under the weight of the vast war debt left by the Second World War," as national parks historian John Ise describes post-war circumstances, "Congress was in no mood to spend lavishly, particularly for the protection of natural resources."[3]

Fortunately, conditions for Texas parks only improved, and upon his retirement as Baylor University president in January 1948, Pat Neff lobbied the parks board to spend some $50,000 on Mother Neff park improvements. Part of his appeal lay in a repeated offer to bequeath his own 2,200-acre spread to the board, putting it next in line after his two children to inherit the land he assembled from Depression-victim farms. Neff had, in effect, already pooled management of the two operations by employing the Jones family. The parks board from its earliest years had arranged such deals, providing low keeper's salary but year-round residence to a family who would open their state park only during the May-through-September season.

Thus what might seem a conflict of interest for the Jones family actually suited the parks board, and of course the ex-governor as well. Neff refocussed his energies on the park following his Baylor retirement. During an April 1948 tour of his Coryell County domain with Harry Provence, managing editor of the *Waco Tribune-Herald*, seventy-six-year-old Neff painted a

glorious picture of the land reclaimed and a native son exhila-
rated. "About 30 minutes from Waco," Provence wrote of their
drive, "the road crested and before [us] spread the greening panorama of the Leon Valley—forests of cedar, oak, pecan and cot-
tonwood rolling down to the river and up the other side to the
horizon. It was age-old beauty. Almost at the river, the entrance
to Mother Neff Park nestled under twin oaks, huge and sprawling in their Spring greenery."

Neff started their tour at the park, demonstrating that "[h]e
knows every tree by its first name," Provence observed. "Down
by the river," he continued, "away from the neat stone and hewn
timber buildings put up by the CCC, is the first building ever
erected in the park." They visited the tabernacle, envisioned in
Isabella Neff's will and constructed in 1925 by state convicts,
where beams and rafters still featured "mottos selected by Pat
Neff and painted there to edify the crowds which once stood
under its shelter. 'I daresay more distinguished speakers have
appeared here than anywhere else in Texas outside the Capitol
in Austin,'" Neff interjected.

The tour continued with Claude Jones escorting in a red
pickup, which along with Neff's six tractors and a bulldozer
must not have been available for park use when Norfleet Bone
earlier observed the need. The gentleman farmer rumbled away
from the park to Neff's own property, pointing to fields of maize,
vetch and sudan grass, grazed by 200 head of cattle, a handful
of buffalo and countless long-horned goats, one named Jerusa-
lem. "'There's the farm where we all worked so hard,'" Neff
pointed toward the center of his family's original 132-acre homestead. "'Now Claude comes up here with the tractors and plows
it before breakfast,'" the editor quoted. Custodian and patri-
arch both left the impression that spring farm work soon would

be curtailed with the park's seasonal opening. "The Joneses say," Provence concluded, "they won't be able to stir the visitors with a stick from now until frost."[4]

During the summer of 1949, dam construction began downstream from Mother Neff park on the Leon River—the resulting huge new lake would be just north of Belton and west of Temple. Sponsored by the U. S. Army Corps of Engineers, the federal dam project carried a typical dual mission of flood control and water supply for area communities. Within the projected lake's drainage area of 3,560 square miles lay the dormant Camp Hood training area, as well as the lower elevations of Mother Neff State Park. This expensive federal undertaking, other officials soon announced, signaled reactivation of the military base, now named Fort Hood and designed to train armored units for the Korean conflict and a global Cold War against the Soviet Union and its satellites. The new lake would serve this training center once again hosting tens of thousands of soldiers and dependents.

Incredibly, the flood-control aspect of the new Belton Reservoir would not protect Mother Neff park, but instead placed the majority of this Leon River recreation ground within the lake's "conservation storage space" at flood stage. Ironically, completion of the dam in April 1954 coincided with one of the worst prolonged droughts in Texas history, which delayed the inevitable flooding in the park at least for a time. When the Leon River rose again over the next two decades, many damaged structures in the park simply disappeared after the cleanup. Neff's hard-won overnight cottages and any other components built of lumber probably exited during this period.[5]

Global military strategy and weather patterns retreated from front page headlines in state newspaper editions covering the

20th of January 1952, as Texans learned that Pat Morris Neff had passed away in Waco. The venerable Neff—self-styled pioneer and statesman, college-trained teacher and lawyer, personal and professional Baptist, elected and appointed public servant, promoter and purveyor of parks—had figuratively steered his state toward many noble concepts, and literally altered a small piece of Central Texas land to his own noble purposes. Neff's indelible image of starched collar, string tie, and frock coat would remain synonymous with Texas in the 1920s, Baylor University through the Depression and war years, and his mother's homestead that he developed as a park "to the public." Myrtle died the next year in July; their gravestone in Waco's Oakwood Cemetery presents a tall shaft embellished with the lone star, flanked by a quote from the Bible on one side, and Neff's words on the other: "I have worked and wrought as best I could to make Texas a better place in which to live."

Neff's passing marked the end of not one, but several chapters in the history of the park. It certainly represented the end of the Neff era that had spanned almost a century from the time his family first settled the land. It also represented, in effect, a final transfer to the state from the family. Mother Neff made the original donation at her death. Years later, her son enlarged the gift with additional land so that it might be developed as a state park under the guidance of the Civilian Conservation Corps and the National Park Service. In 1939, after the CCC pulled out, the governor formally presented it to the Texas State Parks Board as the newest completed addition to the system. In all these conveyances symbolism was the order, since Pat Neff was always and ultimately in control. With his death, however, the state was finally in charge. It was up to them to build on the Neff family legacy.

Soon after Neff's death one of his successors on the State Parks Board, Frank David Quinn, carried the issue of state parks to the polls in a bid for the state senate. He had joined the agency in 1939 as its second executive secretary right after Neff retired as the board's chairman. Quinn and Neff had become friends through the 1940s as the former gently persuaded the latter to keep Mother Neff State Park free of stray goats and spring weeds, and to turn in his park's financial reports on time. Quinn had left the board's employment in 1945, but had returned four years later as a member appointed by Governor Robert Allen Shivers, shortly after most of the old state historical parks transferred to his agency. While chairman of the board he had lost the senate race, but thrust state parks into a timely statewide forum—much as Neff had done in 1923—and convinced subsequent legislatures of the need for better funding of forty-four parks now in the system.

Beginning in the mid-1950s, the National Park Service at last convinced Congress that its priceless resources and ever-increasing visitation deserved critical funding increases. The bureau's "Mission 66" program resulted, with many lasting improvements and more parklands added to the national park system over the coming decade. Over the same period in Texas, Quinn's efforts resulted in a major turning point in 1963, as Governor John Bowden Connally, Jr. brokered merger of the State Parks Board and the State Game & Fish Commission. Neff's overarching interests while governor in conservation and recreation parks never prompted such a coalition, but for the new Texas Parks & Wildlife Department its fifty-eight-park budget tripled to $1.7 million. Connally's momentum led in 1967 to a $75 million bond issue for parkland acquisition and in 1971 to a cigarette tax collected for development of park facilities.[6]

By the early 1980s the department operated 130 state parks and directed millions of dollars in development at the newest units. Its thirty-one surviving parks from the New Deal era, while affectionately labeled the "backbone of the system," still relied on 50-year-old facilities that endured heavy use only because of their durable construction. Occasional Parks & Wildlife staff repairs and remodelings of CCC buildings emphasized cheap materials and insensitive labor, often with unfortunate results. Mother Neff State Park fared better than many New Deal units during those years. Only its keeper's residence changed appreciably. Originally a duplex filled with custom-made furniture from the CCC shop at Bastrop, it underwent interior conversion to a three-bedroom house.

As with most older day-use parks in the system, Mother Neff, through no concerted effort, gradually reverted to service for a very small region. At least renewed interest in its CCC origins led to annual reunions of surviving enrollees coordinated with Mother's Day observances, bringing occasional visitors from farther away than McGregor and Gatesville. The park seemed to be fading with advancing age, unable to capture a younger audience and uncertain about recovery after the next prolonged flood.

Then one May afternoon in 1990, Coryell County resident Clay Davis, living on Old River Road outside the park's west entrance, drove home beneath his familiar continuous canopy of centuries-old shade trees. At the threshold of Mother Neff's traditional visitor season (though all state parks by then were open year round), Davis suddenly encountered the systematic devastation of huge trees beside the road, and preparation for drilling large holes along the country lane and setting a line of new utility poles. "They came in with over ten trucks," Davis described his shock and anger for a later interview by Baylor University historians, and "twelve to fifteen workmen. My wife . . . said there's limbs all over the road; they're up there cutting the limbs out of those trees." The line crews came from McLennan County Electric Cooperative—direct descendant of the New Deal's rural electrification program—following orders to bypass their old line running behind Davis's residence.

When county commissioners and the state representative could not halt this calamitous project, the attorney general forced temporary suspension of work on the power line. Davis and his neighbors received immediate support from county historians, Baylor officials, Parks & Wildlife staff, and the Texas Historical Commission, all confirming their feelings that Old River Road and Mother Neff State Park possessed enough historical significance to be listed in the National Register of Historic Places. Through this determination, federally funded administrators must cooperate with the state historical commission to explore more sensitive solutions to their routine business. The local electric co-op received funds from the federal Rural Electrification Administration, precisely as it had in the 1930s when President Roosevelt had established the partnership. Davis volunteered to write the National Register nomination, especially since "the power company would not back off," he recalled. "So I was writing history with one hand and fighting the power company with the other."

His efforts galvanized the community in favor of saving the ancient trees, and at the same time brought new appreciation for the roadway and Mother Neff State Park. Davis unearthed the long-forgotten story of Pat Neff's repeated

efforts to build the river road and to incorporate its picturesque right-of-way into the park's management. Davis and
the state historians also put on paper for the first time a comprehensive account of the CCC work at Mother Neff, and
its National Park Service designs for the rustic-style facilities
there. A subsequent district court injunction halted further
destruction along the utility line, and in 1992 Mother Neff
State Park entered the National Register of Historic Places,
the first Texas state park so honored.

Just as the Old River Road victory seemed complete, in
December 1991 unseasonable rains saturated west Central
Texas and filled most of the region's flood-control reservoirs
to capacity, including Belton Lake. As heavy rains continued
through the spring, Mother Neff superintendent Peter Carpenter told the *Waco Tribune-Herald* that the results were the
worst flood in his memory. "I've been here 21 years," he told
the newspaper, "I've seen some 2- or 3-foot floods during
the years, but never anything like this." The park's low-el-
evation public area remained under water for six months,
and at peak inundation in mid-April 1992 "the water stood
22 feet above the park grounds," the article described.

When waters receded that fall, Parks & Wildlife officials
moved immediately to clear roads, picnic grounds, and buildings of silt and debris. Rather than abandon the park to this
crisis, the Austin staff pushed to develop a new master plan.
Mother Neff would be saved and rehabilitated, in part because of the National Register listing and devotion of park
professionals, but primarily because surrounding neighbors
in Bell, Coryell, and McLennan counties came to the park's
rescue through volunteer work and heartfelt appeals for rebuilding.[7]

As the 75th anniversary of Pat Neff's creation of the State Parks Board approached in 1998, Parks & Wildlife planners projected an ambitious rejuvenation of the symbolic "first" park in their system. Even as agency artisans—termed a "force account" crew—rebuilt CCC structures and buildings within the Leon River floodplain and restoration began on the park's upper grassland prairie ecosystem, negotiations advanced for the purchase of some 200 acres just west of the park's high ground, ideal for new recreational development. The existing park's six fully equipped campsites, twenty-five tent sites, and some twenty-five picnic tables in the floodplain could then be supplemented with an equal number of outdoor facilities far from future floods. And the property offered for sale by park neighbors could accommodate a new thoroughfare for rerouting through-traffic on the Old River Road, to eliminate this disruption for park patrons.

Of projected $3.5 million needed to implement this plan, which was developed between 1994 and 1996, about ten percent would cover the high-ground land purchase. But by 1998, the world of state park development in Texas, as Pat Neff might wryly observe, had moved slowly into a phase of introspection rather than expansion. Funds actually could be scheduled for improvements, according to agency planners, but incredibly, no state money was available for land acquisition. Even efforts of the newly formed support group, Friends of Mother Neff State Park, led by neighbor Clay Davis and other advocates, could not collect critical dollars to buy the land and launch the project. The moment was lost, property owners sought other buyers, and the expansion plan was shelved until, perhaps, the world again moves to more favorable conditions.[8]

Nevertheless, in early 1998 the formal commemoration of this 75th birth-year for the Texas state park system began with a bright spotlight—literally—on Isabella Neff, her son Pat, and the recreation park that became their legacy. Actors portraying the venerable mother and son, plus other historic figures from the first State Parks Board, reenacted a condensed series of telling moments from 1921, 1923, and 1925 at the Capitol's senate chamber in Austin.

The Pat Neff character, in starched collar and vested suit, described parks to a backdrop of politicians and onlookers: "Here, on bluebonneted hills and daisy-decked meadows the old grow young, the sick regain health and the weary enjoy a quiet rest." After fulfilling the Isabella Neff-character's wish of preserving their Leon River campground as a "park for the public" by winning his debate with stodgy 1920s legislators, "Governor Neff" approached 1998 Governor George Walker Bush in the audience. "You mind holding this while I'm gone?" the actor inquired of the politician, handing over a copy of the 1923 parks bill. "We'd all be mighty grateful."[9]

Not long after this kick-off for a year-long "Grounds for Celebration" series of official events, the keepers of Mother Neff State Park prepared for another summer season of recreational visitors, as they have for more than three-quarters of a century. Despite an indefinite delay in plans for major expansion and development of facilities, the little park stubbornly endures the passage of time and the inevitable changes on its landscape and its culture.

By the end of the century, in fact, Mother Neff State Park had come full circle, from a shady riverside "beauty spot" to a relatively important unit in the mid-century state-park system, then back to its fundamental role as a community recreation ground. After a series of setbacks and gradual decline from the 1950s through the 1990s, the park has now rediscovered its original purpose, through service primarily to the descendants of local settlers around its perimeter and from nearby towns.

This new generation of Texans, Neff would be the first to understand, has found here a place "to go 'back to nature,' where the bees hum, the birds sing, the brooks ripple, the breezes blow, the flowers bloom and the bass bite."

Epilogue
Legacies of the CCC
at Mother Neff State Park

M other Neff State Park is located on State Highway
236 in eastern Coryell County, approximately fifteen miles east of the county seat, Gatesville. It is
only eight miles west of Moody and twelve miles southwest of
McGregor in McLennan County. Prominent signs on Interstate
35 at Bruceville-Eddy, just south of Waco, direct travelers westward to the park via Farm-to-Market Road 107. Nearby, to the
south of the park, are the growing metropolitan areas of Killeen
and Temple in Bell County. So close is the army's vast Fort Hood
at Killeen, in fact, that rolling echoes of cannon rounds are frequently mistaken by park visitors as thunder, even on cloudless
days.

By whatever route one visits the park, the final approach is
reminiscent of entering an oasis. Rolling prairie land gives way
quickly to the dense woods of the Leon River bottoms and to
the craggy ravines of the stream's immediate drainage system.
Drivers on the state highway are compelled by the topography
and by the design of the road to slow down near the park en-

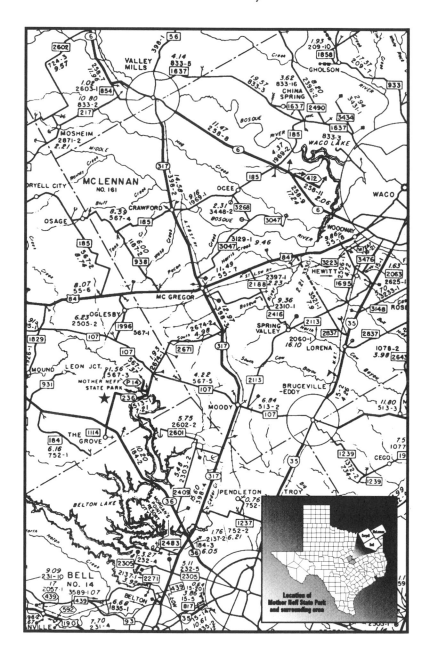

Location of Mother Neff State Park and surrounding area.

trance. There, the first views of the park reveal significant vestiges of the Civilian Conservation Corps, from the low stone
entryway to the central open setting of the original park buildings. But, to those who take the time to investigate the park
further, the story of the boys of 817 unfolds many times over.
This epilogue then will serve as a field guide for those interested
in the cultural landscape the National Park Service and the Civilian Conservation Corps left behind.

Entryway, 1938

Situated on State Highway 236 east of the historic Halbert's
Crossing on the Leon River is the 1938 stone entryway constructed
by the CCC boys as one of the last of their projects in the park. The
entry was initially planned for a site farther north along the highway, and the change in location may have contributed to the delay
in construction. It was not completed by the time Company 817
left in the summer of 1938, so a side camp of CCC boys from
Cleburne was brought in to finish the work.

Two low stone walls, each prominently ending at broad,
battered pylons, flank either side of the main park road. The
horizontality of the entry's design complements the terraced
slopes along the river, while also allowing maximum views of
the central park area. The structure, while impressive in its design and craftsmanship, does not compete with the pavilion's
architecture, clearly visible over a hundred yards beyond. The
alignment of the road and the angle of the entryway visually
draw visitors away from the highway and into the park.

Pavilion, 1937-38

Referred to in early records as the tabernacle, the massive,
open-sided pavilion is the dominant CCC structure immedi-

ately visible from the entryway. As originally designed and built, it was flanked by wide-timbered pergolas resting on squared stone pillars at the corners. Smaller columns provided additional support across the lengthwise span. The lower wooden elements of the pergolas have since been lost to floods, which at times covered major portions of the pavilion. Remnants of the pergola support columns and bases can still be seen.

The loss of the side arcades, or aisles, of the pergolas has altered the building's original horizontal massing, but the design remains evocative of the natural caves and limestone ledges found in the park and elsewhere along the Leon. A key feature in that regard is the impressive archway that dominates the eastern facade and provides the visual replication of a weathered rockshelter. Massing of the eastern gabled end of the structure is enhanced by hefty stone pilasters on either side of the arch. Small lighting fixtures, crafted by the metalworking crews of the CCC, add to the overall feeling of mass and permanence.

The west end of the structure was originally enclosed with a backdrop for a performing stage. Furnishings included both chairs and heavy pews constructed of native timbers by the CCC camp at Bastrop State Park. Many of the furnishings went the way of flood waters over the years, but remaining ones have been used to replicate replacements. Overhead, the massive timber framing, joined with metal braces, contributes to the rustic feel of the architecture.

The pavilion is located directly on the raised former roadway of Halbert's Crossing, and remnants of the bridge abutment can be found on the riverbank behind the building. The significant man-made terrace flanking the pavilion is not easily discerned because it blends so well with the surrounding landscape, but in the 1930s the impressive earth-moving project brought sightseers from many neighboring towns and communities. The purpose of the terrace was to elevate the surrounding grounds above the known flood level, and it served that function reasonably well until the construction of Lake Belton on the Leon River put the pavilion deeper into the potential path of rising waters.

Site of the Neff Family Pavilion, ca. 1920s

Southwest of the entryway and south of the pavilion is the site of the Neff family pavilion, a frame structure that served as the focal point of community gatherings, family reunions, church revivals, and country chautauquas in the years before the coming of the CCC. It was the building that Pat Neff adorned with vivid painted symbols and the motivational slogans he hoped would serve as a source of inspiration and inner reflection for his park guests.

The frame pavilion that marks the site today is not the original structure and, while neither was constructed by the CCC, the location was used by the boys of Company 817 as a stone-finishing area. Large limestone rocks from several nearby quarries were delivered by truck to the pavilion, where crews of young men shaped them into smaller, ashlar-cut stones for use in various construction projects throughout the park. From the site of the early pavilion, visitors can see two significant examples of the boys' stonework—the CCC pavilion and the clubhouse—and appreciate how much effort went into turning boulders to building stones.

Clubhouse, May 1935-March 1937

The stone and timber clubhouse is the companion formal facility to the pavilion. Horizontal in design and tucked off to the north of the central flagpole circle on another man-made terrace, the building has assumed a secondary role with regard to the primary view corridor from the entryway. It was built before the pavilion, however, and was originally designed to be the primary center of both park business and recreation. The building houses a number of rooms, which were first used for office and concession space, a breezeway, where early dances and other entertainment functions were held, a large stone fireplace, an interior fireplace, a partial basement, and restrooms. Although the building conformed to overall design guidelines of the National Park Service in the 1930s, it remains distinctive in its cruciform floorplan and interior space alignment.

The breezeway and fireplace features, which Pat Neff found so objectionable because he believed them to be more stylistic than functional—and therefore certainly not designed by Texans—provided the refectory space common in other NPS/CCC parks. The trans-axis alignment, which visually works against the fireplace as a focal point, gives the area the feel of a hallway or open passage. Regardless, the open roof timbers, iron joinery, heavy metal light fixtures, and massive Adirondack-style furniture, provide a warm, intimate feeling ideal for small gatherings.

Significant architectural elements of the building include the cruciform floorplan, stone window sills, timbered lintels, gabled rooflines, stone arches, and a flagstone breezeway floor with a lone star detail. The clubhouse, also referred to as the combination building and the concession building, provided office space for park personnel until the time of the devastating 1991 flood. Water rose so quickly during that time, and without sufficient warning, that the staff was unable to remove important records and archives before they were inundated. When the waters finally receded, offices were relocated to portable quarters within the park so they could be more easily removed in the event of subsequent flooding.

Camp Bell, 1935

The large iron bell located near the flagpole in the central park circle was donated to the boys of Company 817 by Charles Chapin, who farmed nearby land in the 1930s. Originally located at the site of the CCC camp in the upper reaches of the park, the bell was used to summon enrollees for all sorts of gatherings, from reviews and retreats to meals and safety drills. It remained at the camp location until the 1980s, when former enrollees moved it to its present site.

Park Scenic Road, 1935-1936

The scenic park road reaches from the lower entryway area, skirting steep ravines and passing through dense woodlands en route to the open prairies of the upper parkland. Along the way, it passes over a number of small, rock-lined culverts built by the CCC to direct drainage under the roadway. The culverts, like other rustic features of the park landscape, are designed to merge visually with the surroundings, but the careful visitor can follow the contours of visible drainages and note the presence of stone-lined basins along the road. These basins funneled water to the culverts.

Along the road, pulloffs provide access to Tonkawa Cave, the park's trail system, and the Wash Pond (see below). The scenic road loops at its upper terminus, where park staff have provided access to meadow trails. CCC enrollees planted some of the vegetation in the area, especially many of the junipers that still dot the landscape.

Of particular importance to understanding the amount of work that went into the construction of the scenic road is the realization that it did not exist prior to the coming of the CCC. NPS officials designed the road to meander along the ravines and escarpments, and frequently the land had to be severely contoured to accommodate the concept. CCC workers used dynamite to blast rock from certain areas and then spent countless hours hauling more rock to buttress sharp curves, to line drainages, and to provide barriers and pulloffs. The scenic road, which appears both natural and ancient, was one of the major construction projects within the park during the CCC years.

Tonkawa Cave, excavated 1935

When CCC workers at the creekside rockshelter site came across the buried remains of a skeleton, believed to be those of an Indian, park superintendent C. R. Byram directed excavations of the shelter's floor. His efforts resulted in the recovery of numerous lithic artifacts, as well as another skeleton and possibly part of a third. Byram, who was not a trained archaeologist or anthropologist, speculated that the burial was that of a Tonkawa Indian and that it included evidence of cannibalism. Given the presence of stone implements, however, it is more likely the skeletons were of much greater antiquity.

Byram enthusiastically allowed the enrollees to display the human remains and stone artifacts for a time in the camp museum, where they were photographed for a special edition of the *Blue Eagle News,* before being returned to their burial site in the cave. Camp workers crafted a metal plaque to mark the location, but it was later stolen, along with the remains, by looters.

Tonkawa Cave, more precisely a natural rockshelter formed by eons of flowing waters moving against the limestone ledge of the bank, figured prominently in early plans for the park. It was to be a primary picnic area, complete with rustic stone tables and a barbecue pit. It was during construction of those facilities that the bodies were uncovered. Despite the interruption of the impromptu excavations, work on the picnic facilities continued and were eventually completed. The cave's improvements were later removed to allow for a more natural setting, but evidence of the barbecue pit, as well as the stone steps on both sides of the shelter, can still be seen.

Tonkawa Cave remains one of the park's most popular features. The dramatic setting, below the scenic road and well above the small stream that helped carve the natural feature, provides visitors a glimpse of what life was like for the indigenous people who made their home throughout the area centuries ago. Tonkawa Cave is one of several archaeological features within the park that are protected by both state and federal laws. Visitors are reminded to leave any artifacts—historic or prehistoric—in situ, as they are found. The preservation of protected sites, including the constructed features of the CCC, is essential to the long-term integrity and interpretation of the park.

The Wash Pond, 1936

Located along the main trail system that follows Wash Pond Creek is a natural basin that Pat Neff believed was used by both Indians and pioneer settlers as an important source of fresh water. CCC workers enhanced the site by raising the level of the natural dam in order to enlarge the pool. Still discernible in the cement of the dam is an inscription denoting the work of the CCC.

Observation Tower, 1935-1936

Near the center of the park and in back of the superintendent's house is a large cylindrical observation tower. Built of stone veneer over a hollow metal core, it originally disguised a water tank. The structure is situated along the park's highest elevation, providing visitors with sweeping vistas of the entire park and surrounding land. Hikers can reach the tower from the central trail system.

The observation tower was constructed on a tiered foundation of fieldstone. The stonework on the structure is, in contrast, more refined, although random in size and texture. A curved set of stairs flanked by a decorative iron balustrade, provides access to the top.

Foot Trails, 1935-1937

A series of short trails combine into an overall system that reaches from the lower park area, along a stream, through the Tonkawa Cave area, and up to the observation tower. Although used extensively, the trails have remained very narrow and unobtrusive. Where they cross steep slopes, CCC workers fitted large stones into the pathway, using meandering patterns that replicated natural outcroppings of the area.

Picnic Areas, 1935-1937

Throughout the park are isolated picnic units, consisting of massive stone tables and flanking seats. There were also concrete and stone barbecue pits, although many have been removed for fire safety considerations. The picnic units are constructed of fieldstone, which provides a more rustic, and therefore less intrusive, feel. Park usage patterns have changed over the years, and some of the picnic units are now somewhat isolated, but their simple architecture serves as an important reminder of the organic design objectives that guided the NPS during the days of New Deal park development.

Site of the CCC Camp, 1934-1938

Located in fields north of the superintendent's house and immediately adjacent to State Highway 236 is the site of the CCC camp for Company 817. A makeshift village of barracks and rock-lined lanes, it was home for hundreds of boys and workers from late 1934 to the summer of 1938. Here, the boys were awakened by reveille to assemble at the central flagpole for posting of the colors each morning. They ate their meals at the mess tent, relaxed in the recreation hall, and played football, baseball, and basketball in adjacent fields, where surface stones caused more than an occasional bruise. Each evening they retired early for much-needed sleep. Their personal space was defined by a bunk and a trunk, or a locker, in multiple-boy cottages whose thin walls and minimalist construction afforded little relief from the outside climate. It was in this camp village that many of the boys from rural Texas farms saw electric lights for the first time or heard the scratchy but magical sounds of a radio. From the camp, they left each morning for their work details where they quarried rock, built roads and trails, and crafted magnificent architecture. And, it was on this hill that many of the boys formed friendships that lasted lifetimes.

Archaeological investigations at the site of the CCC camp, conducted with the aid of historic photographs and other archival data, have located remains of trails and building alignments barely discernible in the rocky soils and dense field vegetation. Such investigations prove that even temporary activities such as the camp can leave lasting imprints on the land.

Caretaker's House, 1937-1938

The first caretaker facilities were located in the clubhouse, but work on a separate residence began in 1937. The present structure represents a compromise from the original conceptual plans, which called for both the caretaker's house and separate guest quarters. Over Pat Neff's objections, the two were eventually combined, with only a single room, a bath, and a garage area set aside for special guests. Over the years, that public space has been incorporated into the superintendent's living quarters, and other elements of the original design have been extensively altered in an effort to modernize the home. Regardless, the structure contributes to the overall park architecture in basic design. Its stonework, especially, represents the characteristic nature of the NPS design found in the other park structures.

The Old River Road, 1939

Pat Neff personally lobbied for construction of the scenic road that provides access to the west side of the park. Known locally as the Old River Road because it partially follows the meanders of the Leon River, it is officially the Oglesby-Neff Park Road. Few visitors, or even area residents, are aware of its significant history. Funding for its construction came from federal road and relief programs. It was officially marked and designated as Texas F. A. S. (federally assisted secondary) Road 21-B(1). That historical fact largely passed from the public consciousness in later years, and certainly was not remembered by subsequent generations who used and maintained the route. When the scenic and historic integrity of the route was threatened by plans to remove trees in favor of utility poles, however, research by Clay Davis, a resident of the Old River Road, uncovered its celebrated past and its association with both Pat Neff and the CCC. As a result, the historic road was listed, along with the park, on the National Register of Historic Places.

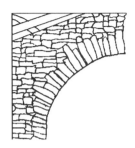

Notes

Preface: Roaming the Cultural Landscape

1. James West Davidson and Mark Hamilton Lytle, *After the Fact: The Art of Historical Detection* (New York: Alfred A. Knopf, 1982), p. 29.

2. *Fort Worth Star-Telegram,* May 19, 1921.

3. W. Somerset Maugham, *The Moon and Sixpence* (New York: The Modern Library, 1919), p. 10.

Chapter 1: Embracing Change

1. Walter Prescott Webb, *The Great Plains* (New York: Grosset and Dunlap, 1931), pp. 8-9.

2. Webb, *The Great Plains*, p. 9.

3. Frederick Jackson Turner, *The Frontier in American History* (New York: Henry Holt and Company, 1920 [1945]), p. 1.

4. Turner, *The Frontier in American History*, p. 12.

5. Frank E. Vandiver, *The Southwest: South or West?* (College Station: Texas A&M University Press, 1975), p. 7.

6. Vandiver, *The Southwest,* pp. 12-13.

7. Vandiver, *The Southwest,* p. 23.

8. Dan K. Utley, Stephen M. Carpenter, S. Chris Caran, and Solveig A. Turpin, *Mother Neff State Park: Prehistory, Parks and Politics.* Texas Parks and Wildlife Cultural Resource Management Report 96-4 (Austin: Texas Parks and Wildlife Department, 1996), pp. 31-33.

9. William W. Newcomb, "Historic Indians of Central Texas," *Bulletin of the Texas Archeological Society, 64,* pp. 1-63; Utley et al., *Mother Neff State Park,* p. 33.

10. Simmons, *History of Mother Neff Memorial State Park* (Gatesville, TX: Freeman Printing Plant, 1949), pp. 10-11; Utley et al., *Mother Neff State Park,* p. 35.

11. Simmons, *History of Mother Neff,* pp. 58-59; General Land Office county land files, Austin; Coryell County Deed Records, Office of the County Clerk, Coryell County Courthouse, Gatesville, Texas.

12. Emma Morrill Shirley, "Mother Neff Park—The Mother of the Entire Texas Park System." Unpublished and undated manuscript in the Pat Neff Papers, Texas Collection, Baylor University, p. 2.

13. Charles W. Ramsdell, "The Natural Limits of Slavery Expansion," *Mississippi Valley Historical Review 16* (2): 151-171.

14. Pat M. Neff, *The Battles of Peace* (Fort Worth: Pioneer Publishing Company, 1925), p. 209.

15. Shirley, "Mother Neff Park," p. 1.

16. Neff, *Battles of Peace,* p. 215.

17. Neff, *Battles of Peace,* p. 215.

18. "Isabella Neff Started State Parks in Texas," *St. Louis Post-Dispatch*, December 27, 1925.

Chapter 2: A Mother's Will and a Son's Way

1. Thomas E. Turner, "Neff, Pat Morris," in Ron Tyler et al., eds., *The New Handbook of Texas*(Austin: Texas State Historical Association, 1996).

2. James Wright Steely, *See Texas First: The dream of a state park system from San Jacinto to Longhorn Cavern, 1883-1932*, unpublished manuscript, 1997.

3. Lewis L. Gould, *Progressives and Prohibitionists: Texas Democrats in the Wilson Era* (Austin: Texas State Historical Association, 1992).

4. Ralph W. Steen, "Ferguson, James Edward," in Tyler et al., *The New Handbook of Texas*.

5. Gould, *Progressives and Prohibitionists*, pp. 271-278; Norman Brown, *Hood, Bonnet, and Little Brown Jug, Texas Politics, 1921-1928* (College Station: Texas A&M University Press, 1984, pp. 12, 15-16); Seth McKay, *Texas Politics* (Lubbock: Texas Tech Press, 1952), p. 93.

6. Steely, *See Texas First*; Brown, *Hood, Bonnet, and LittleBrown Jug*, pp. 12-13; Neff, *The Battles of Peace*, pp. 13-17.

7. "Mrs. Isabella Neff, Governor's Mother, Dies at Executive Mansion," *San Antonio Express*, May 19, 1921.

8. McLennan County Clerk's Office, Wills, File E/5641; see also Probate Minutes, Wills, vol. 19, pp. 206-208, item no. 52; see also Probate Minutes, vol. 20, pp. 374-375. Attorney John E. Williams, while employed as a planner by Texas Parks & Wildlife Department, explained to the authors that "to the public" is common language in legal documents for dedication of land to county governments, most often for road easements; official letter, February 28, 1995.

9. Steely, *See Texas First*.

10. *Amarillo News*, June 25 and *Dallas Morning News*, June 28, 1922, both quoted in Emma Morrill Shirley, "The Administration of Pat M. Neff: Governor Of Texas 1921-25," A. J. Armstrong, ed., *The Baylor Bulletin*, 41/4, December 1938, pp. 67-69.

11. Steely, *See Texas First*; "Neff Urges State System of Parks; Governor in Special Message Says Texans Must 'Go Back to Nature,' " *Dallas News*, May 2, 1923.

12. "State Parks," in Neff, *Battles of Peace,* pp. 127-135; *General Laws of The State of Texas Passed By The Thirty-Eighth Legislature At Its Second Called Session* (1923), pp. 58-60.

13. Steely, *See Texas First;* "See Texas First," *Texas Highway Bulletin*, July 1924; "Park Seekers Find Thrilling Scenery," *Galveston News*, July 24,1924.

14. D. E. Colp letter to Mrs. W. C. Martin, October 24, 1924; Colp to Oscar Dancy, October 27, 1924; all D. E. Colp Papers, Barker Texas History Collections (hereinafter referred to as BTHC).

15. D. E. Colp letter to Austin North, January 2, 1925, BTHC.

16. "State Acquires 42 Tracts For Parks," *Dallas News*, January 19, 1925.

17. "Gifts To Be Declined With Thanks," *Dallas News*, January 21, 1925.

18. Steely, *See Texas First*; Neff to Colp, October 11, 1926, BTHC.

19. Colp letter to Neff, March 29, 1927, BTHC.

20. "Annual Chautauqua Mother Neff Park," *Waco Farm and Labor Journal*, July 13, 1928. Pat Neff Papers, Texas Collection, Baylor University.

21. Ferguson telegram to Neff, April 28, 1933; Neff tele-

gram to Ferguson, April 29, 1933, Texas Collection, Baylor University; *Senate Journal*, 39th Legislature (1925), p. 18.

Chapter 3: Building a Park

1. John A. Salmond, *The Civilian Conservation Corps: A New Deal Case Study, 1933-1942* (Durham: Duke University Press, 1967), p. 30.

2. *Civilian Conservation Corps: What It Is and What It Does* (Washington: CCC Office of the Director, 1941), p. 6.

3. T. H. Watkins, *The Great Depression: America in the 1930s* (Boston: Little, Brown and Company, 1993), p. 130.

4. Salmond, *Civilian Conservation Corps,* pp. 121-127.

5. Salmond, *Civilian Conservation Corps,* p. 30.

6. Leslie Alexander Lacy, *The Soil Soldiers: The Civilian Conservation Corps in the Great Depression* (Radnor, PA: Chilton Book Company, 1976), pp. 101-102.

7. Robert L. Nettles. Oral history interview with Dan K. Utley, July 13, 1994.

8. Nettles, interview.

9. Nettles, interview.

10. Nettles, interview.

11. Nettles, interview; Thomas F. Prater, Jr. Oral history interviews with Dan K. Utley, June 15-16, 1993. Transcripts in process, Institute for Oral History, Baylor University, Waco, Texas; Edwin Hill, *In the Shadow of the Mountain: The Spirit of the CCC* (Pullman: Washington University Press, 1990), p. 47.

12. Burt M. Gillis. Oral history interview with Dan K. Utley, July 8, 1994.

13. Nettles, interview.

14. A. L. Gibbs. Oral history interview with Dan K. Utley, July 15, 1994.

15. *Civilian Conservation Corps: What It Is and What It Does*, p. 7.

16. *Blue Eagle News*, April 14, 1935.

17. Company 817, Civilian Conservation Corps annual, 1936, p. 49; *Blue Eagle News*, April 13, 1938.

18. *Blue Eagle News*, September 16, 1934.

19. *Blue Eagle News*, December 9, 1934.

20. *Blue Eagle News*, January 6, 1935.

21. James Wright Steely, "Rustic Style in Depression Texas: Federal Architecture in the State Parks, 1933-1941." Master's thesis, The University of Texas at Austin, 1985.

22. Quoted in Steely, "Rustic Style," p.24.

23. Herbert Maier. Undated speech. Pat M. Neff papers, Texas Collection, Baylor University, Waco, pp.1-2.

24. Maier, n.d., pp. 3-4.

25. Steely, "Rustic Style," pp. 96-99.

26. *Waco Tribune-Herald*, November 22, 1941; George Colias. Oral history interview, transcript in process, Institute for Oral History, Baylor University, Waco, Texas.

27. *San Antonio Express-News*, June 29, 1965. Obituary of Walter K. Adams.

28. SP-38 Report to the National Park Service, December 3, 1935; *Blue Eagle News*, January 3, 1935.

29. SP-38 Report to the National Park Service, October 12, 1935.

30. SP-38 Report to the National Park Service, October 12, 1935.

31. *Blue Eagle News*, March 24, 1935.

32. *Blue Eagle News*, April 14, 1935.

33. Simmons, *History of Mother Neff*, p. 61.

34. Nettles, interview.

35. *Blue Eagle News*, July 21, 1935.

36. *Blue Eagle News*, July 21, 1935.

37. *Temple Telegram*, May 28, 1938.

38. Letter from Pat M. Neff to George Nason, Herbert Maier, Conrad Wirth, and D. E. Colp, October 12, 1935. Neff correspondence files, Texas Collection, Baylor University.

39. Neff to Nason et al., October 12, 1935.

40. Neff to Nason et al., October 12, 1935.

41. *Blue Eagle News*, October 13, 1935; SP-38 Report to National Park Service, January 28, 1935.

42. *Blue Eagle News*, October 6, 1935, March 20, 1936, and April 3, 1936.

43. Letter from Gibb Gilchrist to Pat Neff, September 15, 1936. Neff correspondence files, Texas Collection, Baylor University.

44. *San Antonio Express-News*, May 30, 1965; *Beeville Bee-Picayune*, June 3, 1965.

45. Comments by H. H. Cornell, National Park Service, February 11, 1937. Neff correspondence files, Texas Collection, Baylor University.

46. Letter from Herbert Maier to William J. Lawson, March 2, 1937. Neff correspondence files, Texas Collection, Baylor University.

47. Clay J. Davis. Oral history interview with Dan K. Utley, June 23, 1994. Transcript in process, Baylor University Institute for Oral History, Waco, Texas.

48. Letter from Pat M. Neff to Herbert Maier, July 3, 1937. Neff correspondence files, Texas Collection, Baylor University.

49. Letter from William J. Lawson to B.A. Tripp, December 13, 1937. Neff correspondence files, Texas Collection, Baylor University.

50. Lawson to Tripp, December 13, 1937.

51. *Blue Eagle News*, July 25, 1937.

52. Nettles, interview.

53. Letter from Pat M. Neff to William J. Lawson, July 1, 1938. Neff correspondence files, Texas Collection, Baylor University.

54. Bill Denton. Oral history interview with Dan K. Utley, June 10, 1995.

Chapter 4: Camp Life

1. Salmond, *Civilian Conservation Corps,* p. 4.

2. Letter from Col. Duncan Major to Louis Howe, April 11, 1933, quoted in Salmond, *Civilian Conservation Corps,* p. 49.

3. Eldon Stephen Branda, ed., *The Handbook of Texas: A Supplement* (Austin: The Texas State Historical Association, 1976), p. 642.

4. SP-38 Report to the National Park Service, December 3, 1935.

5. Burt M. Gillis. Oral history interview with Dan K. Utley, July 8, 1994.

6. *Corpus Christi Times*, April 18, 1937.

7. Salmond, *Civilian Conservation Corps,* pp. 149-150.

8. *Blue Eagle News*, October 6, 1934 and January 27, 1935.

9. *Blue Eagle News*, January 27, 1935.

10. *Blue Eagle News*, April 28, 1935.

11. *Blue Eagle News*, January 27, 1935

12. *Blue Eagle News*, April 21, 1935.

13. Jed H. Taylor, *Organization of Civilian Conservation Corps Camp Library-Reading Rooms* (Washington: American Association for Adult Education, 1938), pp. 28-42.

14. *Blue Eagle News*, June 27, 1936.

15. Marlys Rudeen, *The Civilian Conservation Corps Camp Papers: A Guide* (Chicago: The Center for Research Libraries, 1991), pp. 8-468.

16. James S. Olson, ed., *Historical Dictionary of the New Deal: From Inauguration to Preparation for War* (Westport, CT: Greenwood Press, 1985), p. 362.

17. *Blue Eagle News*, April 7, 1935.

18. *Blue Eagle News*, April 7, 1935.

19. *Blue Eagle News*, June 2, 1935 and May 12, 1935.

20. *Blue Eagle News*, July 28, 1935.

21. *Blue Eagle News*, January 31, 1936.

22. *Blue Eagle News*, September 23, 1934.

23. Gillis, interview.

24. *Blue Eagle News*, January 24, 1936.

25. Robert L. Nettles. Oral history interview with Dan K. Utley, July 13, 1994.

26. Gillis, interview.

27. George Carmack and Bonnie Carmack, "Depression-Era Comrades Gather," *Star Magazine, San Antonio Express-News*, September 22, 1984, n.p.

28. *Blue Eagle News*, March 17, 1935.

29. *Blue Eagle News*, February 3, 1935.

30. *Blue Eagle News*, May 12, 1935.

31. *Blue Eagle News*, May 12, 1935; newspaper clipping (no publication noted), May 13, 1935, Pat Neff papers, Texas Collection, Baylor University.

32. *Blue Eagle News*, April 3, 1938.

33. Bill Denton. Oral history interview with Dan K. Utley, June 10, 1995.

34. Carmack and Carmack, "Depression-Era Comrades."

35. *Blue Eagle News*, December 20, 1935.

36. Gillis, interview.

37. Gillis, interview.

38. Gillis, interview.

39. *Blue Eagle News*, January 24, 1935.

40. *Blue Eagle News*, June 20, 1936.

41. *Blue Eagle News*, July 4, 1936.

42. *Blue Eagle News*, February 10, 1937.

43. *Blue Eagle News*, April 10, 1937.

44. *Blue Eagle News*, July 10, 1937.

45. Gillis, interview.

46. Gillis, interview.

47. Arthur M. Schlesinger, Jr., *The Age of Roosevelt.* Vol. 2: *The Coming of the New Deal* (Boston: Houghton Mifflin, 1959), p. 340.

Chapter 5: Politics and a Park

1. *Burnet Bulletin,* August 31, 1939.

2. *Burnet Bulletin,* August 31, 1939.

3. *Abilene Morning News,* April 21, 1935.

4. *Abilene Morning News,* April 21, 1935.

5. Letter from O. T. McGinley to W. R. Poage, April 15, 1938. Neff correspondence files, Texas Collection, Baylor University.

6. McGinley to Poage, April 15, 1938.

7. Letter from Pat M. Neff to Judge Robert Bobbitt, June 29, 1937. Neff correspondence files, Texas Collection, Baylor University.

8. Letter from William J. Lawson to Pat M. Neff, April 11, 1938. Neff correspondence files, Texas Collection, Baylor University.

9. Letter from Pat M. Neff to J. C. Kellam, June 16, 1938, and State Parks Board "traveling expense account," September 16, 1938. Neff correspondence files, Texas Collection, Baylor University.

10. Report by W. F. Ayres, September 15, 1938. Neff correspondence files, Texas Collection, Baylor University.

11. Letter from William J. Lawson to Pat M. Neff, October 16, 1938. Neff correspondence files, Texas Collection, Baylor University.

12. Letter from Pat M. Neff to William J. Lawson, October 31, 1938. Neff correspondence files, Texas Collection, Baylor University.

13. Olson, *Historical Dictionary of the New Deal,* pp. 367-369.

14. Letter from Pat M. Neff to Wendell Mayes, February 29, 1940. Neff correspondence files, Texas Collection, Baylor University.

15. Neff to Mayes, February 29, 1940.

16. Letter from Pat M. Neff to Marie and Tullie Jones, September 13, 1939. Neff correspondence files, Texas Collection, Baylor University.

17. Letter from Pat M. Neff to Claude Jones, September 7, 1939. Neff correspondence files, Texas Collection, Baylor University.

18. Neff to Claude Jones, September 7, 1939.

19. Letters, August 26, 1939, September 7, 1939, September 18, 1939, and September 29, 1939. Neff correspondence files, Texas Collection, Baylor University.

20. Letter from Pat M. Neff to Texas State Parks Board, August 26, 1939. Neff correspondence files, Texas Collection, Baylor University.

21. Neff to Mayes, February 29, 1940.

22. Neff to Mayes, February 29, 1940.

23. Neff to Mayes, February 29, 1940.

24. Letter from Pat M. Neff to Gus Jones, March 6, 1939. Neff correspondence files, Texas Collection, Baylor University.

25. Letter from Pat M. Neff to McGregor Chamber of Commerce and McGregor Rotary Club, June 13, 1939. Neff correspondence files, Texas Collection, Baylor University.

26. Letter from Mrs. A. L. Lee to Pat M. Neff, March 3, 1942. Neff correspondence files, Texas Collection, Baylor University.

27. Letter from Pat M. Neff to Mrs. A. L. Lee, March 7, 1942. Neff correspondence files, Texas Collection, Baylor University.

28. Letter from Pat M. Neff to State Parks Board, August 13, 1943. Neff correspondence files, Texas Collection, Baylor University.

29. Letter from Pat M. Neff to Norfleet G. Bone, August 31, 1945. Neff correspondence files, Texas Collection, Baylor University.

Chapter 6: Back to Nature

1. All 1937 park visitor figures from *The Highland Lakes of Texas: A Study Prepared Under the Authority of the Park, Parkway and Recreational Study Act of June 1936* (Washington, DC: Department of the Interior, 1940), copy at Texas State Archives; May 1945 compilation state park visitor figures from Guy Carlander Papers, Panhandle-Plains Historical Museum.

2. Correspondence and reports from August 1945 between Norfleet G. Bone and Pat Neff, Texas Collection, Baylor University; "McGregor, Texas" and "Killeen, Texas," in Walter

Prescott Webb, ed., *The Handbook of Texas* (Austin: Texas State Historical Association, 1952), and Ron Tyler et al., eds., *The New Handbook of Texas* (Austin: Texas State Historical Association, 1996).

3. 49th Legislature, Regular Session (1945), *General And Special Laws,* pp. 897-904, *Senate Journal*, p. 1297; State Parks Board Minutes, June 24-25, October 5-7, 1945; Conrad Wirth, *Parks, Politics, and the People* (Norman: University of Oklahoma Press, 1980), pp. 47, 225-227, 233; Edwin C. Bearrs, "Arno B. Cammerer 1883-1941," in William H. Sontag and Linda Griffen, eds., *The National Park Service: A Seventy-Fifth Anniversary Album* (Washington, DC: National Park Service, 1990), pp. 38-39; John Ise, *Our National Park Policy: A Critical History* (Baltimore: Johns Hopkins University Press, 1961), p. 455.

4. Harry Provence, "Nature's Academy—Fresh Plowed Soil, Green Grass—Enrolls Pat M. Neff as Ace Observer," *Waco Tribune-Herald,* April 13, 1948.

5. "Belton Lake" and "Droughts," in Tyler et al., *New Handbook of Texas.*

6. Frank David Quinn papers, Barker Library, especially typed address to National Citizens Planning Conference, June 18, 1959, Memphis, Tennessee; "Texas Parks and Wildlife Department," in Tyler et al., *New Handbook of Texas.*

7. Clay J. Davis, oral history interview with Dan K. Utley, June 23, 1994, transcript in process, Baylor Institute for Oral History, Waco, Texas; Darlene McCormick, "Closed Due To High Water," *Waco Tribune-Herald*, May 30, 1992.

8. Bob Singleton, Texas Parks and Wildlife Department planner. Personal interview with James Steely by telephone, April 9, 1998.

9. Clay Nichols, "Way Down Yonder," script commissioned by Texas Parks & Wildlife Department; "State parks mark 75 years with oratory of Gov. Neff," *Austin American-Statesman,* February 27, 1998.

Bibliographic Essay

The Texas government's first timid steps in creating state parks are revealed in yellowing time capsules of legislative journals from the 1880s through the 1940s. Volumes of the *Journal of the House of Representatives* and *Journal of the Senate* for each legislative session are available at the State Capitol's Legislative Reference Library, plus the Texas State Archives in the Capitol Complex and the Barker Collections at the University of Texas at Austin's Center for American History. Indexes vary from year to year in these incredible hand-held monuments to politics and the printing profession, sometimes listing "parks, state parks," or the individual park names as single references to the topic. Of related interest are the laws enacted by each biennial and special session, condensed to volumes confirming legislation that ultimately passed in each session, with budgets appropriate to fund those actions.

The Legislative Reference Library also contains individual state agency biennial reports and audits, including those for the Board of Control after 1919, and the State Parks Board after

1934. Minutes of the State Parks Board, beginning in the summer of 1933 after federal New Dealers encouraged such efficiency, are found at the State Archives, and on microfilm at Texas Parks and Wildlife Department headquarters, 4200 Smith School Road in Austin.

The Barker Collections at UT Austin yield card-catalog subject references to parks by their individual names, often identifying regional magazine and journal articles in the library's extensive holdings. Vertical-file titles on many early recreation grounds, including Mother Neff Park, contain clippings, brochures, and other details on site histories. Fortunately, many years ago someone—records do not reveal who—donated the surviving papers of David Edward Colp, first and longtime chairman of the State Parks Board. Colp's personal files constitute the only consistent record of parks board activities from establishment in 1923 through the New Deal introduction in 1933. Much original correspondence between Colp and Governor Pat Neff on the subjects of good roads, parks, and the little campground on the Leon River fills these largely unorganized boxes.

Since the Civilian Conservation Corps represented the federal government's response to the Great Depression, faithful New Dealers in the field regularly reported project activities to higher authorities in Washington, DC. When the CCC inspector visited Company 817 at Mother Neff State Park, for example, he recorded enrollment statistics and camp conditions, including water quality, daily menus, and the recreation hall's pitiful cash balance. The National Park Service fielded its own inspectors, who submitted monthly summaries of progress on Mother Neff and all other projects sponsored by federal park officials. And individual project superintendents, including C. R. Byram at the Leon River endeavor, submitted periodic written reports on their progress, with priceless photographic snapshots of park construction. All these incredible records are now preserved at the National Archives and Records Administration's facility just outside Washington, DC, in College Park, Maryland.

In Texas, the most extensive archival collection of materials related to the Mother Neff project can be found in the Pat M. Neff papers of the Texas Collection at Baylor University. Neff, the former president of the Waco school who often showed that institution the same kind of proprietary oversight he did his family's park, left a remarkable set of personal papers. Neff was a prodigious letter and speech writer, and a review of both forms of self-expression reveal much about both the personal and the private sides of the man. They were not always the same.

In addition to correspondence, the Neff papers include an impressive collection of local newspaper articles, some of which were generated by Neff himself, as evidenced by extant copies of press releases. The governor and school president are the subject of many, but there are also revealing articles about the Mother Neff project, the work of the Civilian Conservation Corps and the National Youth Administration, the early camp chautauquas, and the park's use for a myriad of community gatherings. Pat Neff knew public relations, and even marketing, and his personal interest in the park is reflected in most of the articles that promoted the site through the 1930s and 1940s. Unfortunately, not all of the provenience survives for the clippings, which sometimes makes the collection difficult for researchers, but relative inferences and chronologies can often be used to provide a context, even where a specific date or publication is unknown.

Complementing the correspondence and clippings of the Neff collection are numerous photographs of the park, most taken in the transitional post-CCC era when Neff was both overseer and promoter. There are also a number of speeches and articles from other individuals representing important aspects of emerging park philosophies at the national level. Neff clearly made the association between his rural park, for example, and the benefits of the automobile era, recreational tourism, and the development of parks across the country. He viewed Mother Neff not only as a beneficiary of such movements, but an integral player as well. Contrasting the articles from his files with his public speeches, it is easy to see the influences.

Research on any historical site must include an in-depth review of local records, primarily those found in county courthouses. Important public records in the offices of county and district officials include deeds, tax abstracts, maps and plats, probate papers, and proceedings from both political and judicial bodies. In the case of the Mother Neff investigations, the review of records in Coryell County, where the Neff family was located, and McLennan County, where Neff maintained his permanent residence, proved both necessary and beneficial. In the local records can be found the legal documentation that helps to explain sequences and to clarify details of events and actions that may have been forgotten or confused over time through reminiscence.

When used properly as a complementary resource, recorded memory is an ideal methodology for social and cultural history, especially as it focuses on feelings, emotions, personal stories, and family histories. Within the reminiscences of those who lived through the stories contained in this book, and who shared them openly with the authors, are the accounts of history that bring out the humor, the relationships, the reflective frames of reference, and the individual actions that are not often found in other records or publications. Oral history has its limitations, as does any methodology, but it is rarely matched for its value in capturing the personal side of a larger story. The oral histories compiled as part of this project were conducted in association with ongoing research projects at the Baylor University Institute for Oral History. When finally transcribed and edited, the memoirs will be deposited in the holdings of the Texas Collection, also at Baylor, where they will be available to both researchers and family members.

With regard to the details and the chronology of CCC camp life at Mother Neff State Park, a remarkable and invaluable resource was the near-complete collection of *Blue Eagle News,* the camp newspaper, at The Center for Research Libraries in Chicago, Illinois. The microfilmed run of the paper begins with the earliest work of Company 817, prior to its association with Mother Neff and continues on a regular basis through the final days of the park project and the unit's existence. Written by the enrollees, the camp papers reveal detailed perspectives on camp programs, projects, discipline, work details, accomplishments, and setbacks, while also preserving stories of camp life, friendships, concerns, and personal growth that are not found in other sources. Throughout the unit and individual histories are the strains of contemporary culture, economics, politics, and values that defined the era of the CCC.

The *Blue Eagle News* was only one of hundreds of CCC newspapers, and the Center for Research Libraries maintains possibly the best national collection of this important historical medium. Any research on the CCC, particularly at the unit level, should include a review of their holdings. The center has produced a finding aid, *The Civilian Conservation Corps Camp Papers: A Guide,* compiled in 1991 by Marlys Rudeen, which provides the newspaper title, the associated company, the historical span of the publication, and the dates of specific holdings. While designed to be a general index, there are details that provide clues to other camp newspapers and projects that prove beneficial to researchers.

Despite the successes and the ubiquitous nature of the CCC, surprisingly few books have presented a broad overview of the organization. The seminal work remains John A. Salmond's *The Civilian Conservation Corps: A New Deal Case Study, 1933-1942* (Duke University Press, 1967). Over thirty years after its publication, it is still the starting point for any research on the CCC. A relatively brief, albeit thorough book, it provides a good general overview of the political history of the CCC, while also focusing attention on camp life, the multiples facets of social experiments, and the realities of outside forces, events, and concerns. Salmond set the standard with his work, and subsequent histories of the CCC have been influenced by his approach and his perspectives.

Another early national overview of the organization is *The Soil Soldiers: The Civilian Conservation Corps in the Great Depression* (Chilton Book Company, 1976) by Leslie Alexander Lacy. As the title implies, Lacy's emphasis is on the conservation side of the CCC equation, but like Salmond, he gives a contextual backdrop for understanding broader objectives of the program.

A good regional overview of the CCC is a chapter entitled, "The Civilian Conservation Corps in the Southwestern United States," in the book, *The Depression in the Southwest* (Kennikat Press, 1980), edited by Donald W. Whisenhunt. The chapter, written by historian Kenneth E. Hendrickson, Jr., gives a local context for the national organization. While not quoted specifically in this work, it remains one of the key resources for any background review on the CCC in Texas.

Much of the historical research on the CCC since Salmond has centered on individual accounts or unit accomplishments. An example is *In the Shadow of the Mountain: The Spirit of the CCC* (Washington University Press, 1990) by Edwin Hill, in which the author details accounts of his service as an enrollee. Similar approaches can be found for the historical treatment of other regions, although most accounts remain limited and are usually found in the form of articles or self-published manuscripts.

For CCC park projects in the Lone Star State, a good basic source is *The Civilian Conservation Corps in Texas State Parks* by James Wright Steely, an author of this publication. The booklet, published by the Texas Parks and Wildlife Department in 1986, gives a brief background history of each of the CCC parks still maintained by the agency. Of particular importance to CCC research are the historic photographs and unit history material it includes.

Hopefully, as this essay and this book will reveal, there are still many aspects of the Civilian Conservation Corps to be explored. Much that has been written to date has centered on politics, and that is understandable given the benchmark status of the Great Depression in our collective history, as well as the dynamism of President Franklin D. Roosevelt and the lasting legacies of his New Deal programs. Unfortunately, as we lose resources, we often realize too late their significance and relevance. There are still many of the CCC "boys" around who can recount their personal views of the program, but their numbers diminish daily. In their memories are the views of the organization from the inside out—views that have too often been neglected, but which are now being preserved by local historical organizations, park personnel, and groups like the National

Association of Civilian Conservation Corps Alumni. Through their efforts, more stories like those centering on one specific park along the Leon River in Central Texas will be passed to future generations of researchers and park enthusiasts.

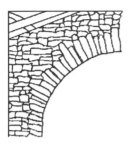

Index